After a degree in Modern History at Oxford University, Patricia Tyerman took a Postgraduate Certificate in Education at the University of London (1970). While teaching in special schools and a child guidance clinic for the Inner London Education Authority, she achieved a First in Psychology and Philosophy from Birkbeck College, University of London (1977). She was a Lecturer and Senior Lecturer in the School of Education at the Open University (1979–99) and she was a senior research fellow at Canterbury Christchurch University (1999–2004).

At the Open University Tyerman co-authored and co-edited six books for a wide readership. Other books include *Inclusion in the City* and *Education in Britain and China*, which were both published by Routledge in 2003. This is her first memoir, written in her maiden name.

Since 2004, Tyerman has written and performed stories for the Spark network at the Canal Café Theatre, London. She has completed creative writing courses run by City University and the Arvon Foundation and belonged to the West9Writers' Group convened by Susan Elderkin, a Granta Best of Young British Novelists (*Sunset Over Chocolate Mountains*, 2000, *The Novel Cure*, 2014).

Tyerman belongs to a weekly writers' group and she divides her time between writing, playing the French Bassoon, seeing her grandsons and exploring London on foot and by bike.

www.patriciatyerman.co.uk

SELF-PORTRAIT WITH PARENTS

HOW ADOLESCENCE GALVANISED ME FOR A SINGLE-BREASTED ADULTHOOD

Patricia Tyerman

SilverWood

Published in 2021 by SilverWood Books

SilverWood Books Ltd
14 Small Street, Bristol, BS1 1DE, United Kingdom
www.silverwoodbooks.co.uk

ISBN 978-1-80042-049-6 (paperback)
ISBN 978-1-80042-050-2 (ebook)

British Library Cataloguing in Publication Data
A CIP catalogue record for this book is
available from the British Library

Page design and typesetting by SilverWood Books

For my sisters and brothers

We each have different perspectives on our upbringing.
This is mine.

Contents

The Sound of Childhood

Tina came round that afternoon, do you remember, Dad? She was neat and wiry in her navy tunic, her hair in dark plaits. I was sturdy in grey corduroys and olive green jumper. We ran to the top of the house.

I did sometimes manage to heave myself up onto the jumping horse in the school gym but I could never execute that flip over to the landing-mat. The lesson came when my thighs slid down the suede flank to a shock of splitting bone. Day and night dissolved into four-hour cycles of codeine and the two-hour spool of a long-playing record – six hundred and seventy two hours dozing in bed in the dining room. *The Mikado* and *Oklahoma* were frescoed into my brain, my left leg shrinking inside its plaster-of-Paris cast. Two weeks on crutches and a final fortnight charging round with rolls of plaster fitted under the cast, then Tina was allowed to come and play. I was so used to my puny but completely functional and painless leg that I didn't give it a moment's thought.

I must have grown since we were last up there, for the hatch up to the attic was now at shoulder height. We stretched and pushed. The square panel creaked open. I had no idea what awaited us. Trying not to look down the gaping stairwell, we used the banister rail to get inside, where a single bulb shed a dim light on floorboards, cobwebs – and nothing. But yes! There was a second, raised doorway. With two months' unspent energy I leapt up.

There was no floor at all in the pitched space, only detached rows of broad joists smelling of earth and stone. The glimmer from the light below encouraged us to tread along the beams, exploring a part of the house I never knew existed. We didn't care if we were walking to the north, south, east or west, we were thrilled by our uncharted steps, bold footprints criss-crossing the dusty space. Suddenly, an explosion of Victorian rubble raged around us and I was flat on my face, spread-eagled across the planks, palms splintered and stinging.

'Whasthathelpwhereareyou?' Tina's words stuck together in the dark. 'Over here,' I coughed. All I could see was a hole between two of the beams.

Inching back on hands and knees, the solid oak now felt fragile and narrow. I had to breathe slowly through pursed lips to keep my balance. We clambered face inwards down through the attics till we arrived back on dry lino. The landing was bathed in a dazzling brightness. My brother's bedroom at the end was a bombed-out shell, a smoky cave, a jagged crater, a storm-cloud of pure matter, its ceiling utterly destroyed. From a distance of more than fifty years, vivid phrases roll freely round my tongue. But back then we froze speechless, though my blood was pumping inside. For how could the slip of one eleven-year-old leg demolish a house? And where was everyone? I don't remember a stampede, or shouting and screaming. I remember silence. Tina must have been sent home and I must have been sent to bed.

My room had a dormer window onto a silver birch tree. I lay under the bedclothes fully dressed, sweating and shivering, listening to the leaves twitching outside, my head and heart racing each other to see which came up with my juiciest fate. Nothing was ever repaired at home, or built from scratch with common tools. How could my crime ever be absolved? And if the house fell down we would all have to move, not only me. I had destroyed my whole family.

In the unnatural calm I heard a rattling, a window or a flap of wallpaper. Except that the noise grew and came closer. It was loud and on the move. Not some devilish Morse code, then, but a familiar three-beat thump. You were climbing the stairs. Holding both your sticks in one hand and gripping the banister with the other. Banging the sticks down on the step above, leaning forward and swinging right leg first, then left leg, up to join them. Sticks, leg, leg. Sticks, leg, leg. The sound that punctuated my childhood. I thought this was how all fathers went up at night.

Instead of going into your room, however, you turned and carried on, climbing up a third flight, to my room. Sticks, leg, leg. Sticks, leg, leg. The once-friendly thudding now sent bullets into my brain. You had never been up to my room. What would you come up for if not for something terrible? And it was taking you so long. Sticks, leg, leg. Sticks, leg, leg. You kicked the door open and leant against the mantelpiece so you could rest your hands and still remain upright. You were breathing hard. The gas fire threw your shadow across the ceiling.

'Alright?' you barked.

What? What did you say? I was shaking with relief. But I felt cheated too. What did you mean was I alright, when the house was falling down? Wasn't this the worst moment in my life? Or in yours? I didn't know of an agreed punishment for house-destruction, but why weren't you furious? Here I was waiting for the lecture, the how-could-you, the New Deal for a very different future. Anything. You didn't even wave your sticks. Did you think your slow journey was fearful enough? You weren't interested in the making or keeping of rules, though, were you? You liked reading aloud, arguing, beating us at cards. From the straightjacket safety of my blankets, I realised we could have killed ourselves. I was unnerved. My cheeks burned. Did you care more about me than the house?

Looking Back

Adolescence

Cancer shocked me into asking how I would cope. I was forty-two. What resilience of mind and body did I have? In the last days of longhand I sat with my notebooks and began to write about my mother and father. Could my early life with them help me through this crisis? My parents were both alive at the outbreak of the First World War. My father grew up in the north-east of England, my mother in the south-east, both of them in families strained by the premature deaths of their fathers, by pre-welfare state money worries and social instabilities, and by tempers and resentments, stifled occasionally to look straight at a camera. My father, scholar turned Fleet Street hero. My mother, who gave up her public and professional life to look after five children and a husband disabled by polio.

My parents retired from London to Suffolk. In the village churchyard their gravestone bears their names and dates and tells me they were man and wife. Nothing more. A small desk sat by the window in my mother's cottage bedroom. The drawer stuck but if you pulled the handle firmly it scraped open. It was full of letters and photographs. I could spread my hands and sift through their loose-leaf history. Now I have corralled this into a personal account of my parents' lives and my relationship to them: the vigour and tension, humour and confusion, noise and stillness. I look back at my young-old self, that large and noisy teenager, enthusiastic when the adjective was still an insult for girls. I face her as she looks back at me. She's the carrier of who I have become. I had no idea how different my feelings about this raw person would become.

Three sisters

A photograph taken in a wintry London back garden in 1952 shows three sisters wearing identical dresses, smocked, with a velvet sash. Party dresses for little girls made for us by Aunty Jessie, our mother's eldest sister. There are ribbons in our hair. The image is black and white but the organza and muslin, light and stiff round our bare legs, was pink and white and pale blue. The photograph I am looking at was taken on our first Christmas Day in the house in West Hampstead. I never think of us like that, three little girls dressed up in identical party dresses. A posed threesome doesn't reflect our regular lives at all. We didn't go about together as a female gang. When we played with Anne she was always the leader, her way of trying to stem the tide of siblings. Sometimes we were her class and she would tell us what to sing. A copy of *Songs of Praise* still has her written instructions at the top of each hymn. On the five-hour car journeys to Suffolk, Anne would be ready with new verses for familiar tunes:

Jim wished to be a pirate in the days of old
killing innocent seamen and stealing bags of gold.

(to the tune of 'Summer Suns are Glowing')

Anne was Angela Rosebud Goldenhair, the first-born beauty, flung from the Essex village of a perfect solo childhood into the crammed chaos of North London.

I make myself look at the summer line-ups of all five of us, taken between 1959 and 1961: three sisters then two brothers all born in the eight and a half years between September 1944 and May 1953. The first two photos were taken in the back garden in West Hampstead and the third in the garden of a seaside cottage in Suffolk. I see a collection of sweet-faced children, with one exception. The boys charm with their baggy grey corduroys and khaki shorts, their fringes, their strappy leather sandals and their big brown eyes. Anne is pretty in her navy polka-dot dress and cream cardigan, or her sky blue slacks and white cotton top, or her royal blue jumper with the sleeves pushed halfway up her arm. Younger sister Mary is gentle and thoughtful in her muted trousers and shirts. Then there's me, the middle sister. In the first picture I am standing there, round cheeks, small mouth and eyes, hair scraped over and held with a Kirby grip, wrinkled red shorts and long thighs. In the second, I have the sense to wear slacks and to tie my hair back more elegantly but now there are breasts which don't yet merit a bra. In these two photos I see that I am the same height as Anne, so the line runs more or less as it should, sloping down from left to right. In the third, however, I have shot up. The line is well and truly disrupted. I still have that full-cheeked, scrunchy-eyed smile and I look happy, four-square. The

Family line-up, 1962

boys are grinning and standing to attention. One sister looks away and the other relaxed. Robert, four years younger than me, was the only one to grow taller, much later. For the whole span of my teenage years, I was the largest in the whole family, men included.

As well as my height and general substance, my behaviour attracted a drastic response. Strategies deployed to maintain space around me had serious lifelong consequences. Anne was bossy, she didn't listen, she smiled in her New Look outfits, she criticised my friends. I was enraged when my mother gave her the fare for both of us if we were going out on a bus together. We fought, in public as well as at home. Between the junior and senior school buildings there was a single playground. I don't remember what exasperated me on that particular day but I do remember a fight when I was eleven and Anne nearly fourteen, a physical scrap with lots of shouting. There wasn't room for both of us.

Yet we would soon be together in the senior school. Our mother was summoned to the headmistress. Anne was sent away. I remember my mother crying on the car journey taking her to boarding school for the first term. Why did she accept this forced separation? It might well have been impossible for us sisters to share space at school as well as at home without causing great sadness and worry for our mother but I don't remember any discussion, any negotiation of a truce. By the age of thirteen or so I was feared as a loose cannon, no longer a girl nor yet a woman but definitely too much.

We three sisters are all left-handed, our brothers both right-handed. Anne and Mary each have a left-handed partner. I ponder that now after my two long relationships with right-handed men. I always notice. Not just the majority of American Presidents but also the woman who once sat opposite me on a train taking left-handed notes from a journal article on 'Traumatic experiences in childhood'. Our father would have been left-handed if he had not had polio. He used to bang his left hand on the table to get rid of persistent pins and needles. As a child in North Yorkshire his older brother Reg was forced to be right-handed. The humiliations Reg endured gave him a stammer that was not attended to until he was in his forties. My cousin Roy remembers Newcastle speech therapist Muriel Morley coming to their house and his father lying on the floor with books under his head. Rather like my relaxation classes before my daughters Joanna and Rachel were born, when we practised deep breathing, then shallow breathing to ride out the pain.

My teenage room

Pearl, the seventeen-year-old in Tessa Hadley's novel *Everything Will Be Alright*, is waiting in her bedroom for friends to come round. Later, they will go out. Reading her story I realised there was nothing in her contemporary room that my teenage self could relate to. On the wall behind the door of my room was a white-painted wooden chest of drawers. On top of this was one of those wooden display cases with two shelves and sliding glass doors, containing dolls-from-around-the-world from travelling parents, aunties and family friends. Then came my mother's childhood upright piano, pretty much unplayable by then. Next to the piano, lengthwise along the next wall, was my bed, covered with a strip of scarlet, ridged cotton. Between the piano and my bed was a stool on which sat a huge walnut-brown radio, powered by two shiny purple valves. I pressed my ears to the dim light of the dial listening to Radio Caroline and BBC serial dramas: Paul Temple with his night train theme tune and his wife Steve, or George Cole as John le Carré's Smiley. Cole's obituaries and other tributes focused on his television roles, particularly Arthur Daley in *Minder*. Has everyone forgotten his rich radio voice? Definitely as good as Alec Guinness.

My room was on a sort of mezzanine level. Not the attic proper, but still somehow above most of the house. The window, in the middle of the wall opposite the door, was cut into the slope of the roof. Outside, a patch of lead lay flat between triangles of siding. In summer, I could climb out and smell the swishing birch tree only a few feet away by the garden fence. I set a waste-paper basket on fire out there. I can't remember if this was deliberate or, if it was, what I was burning. Perhaps I lost patience with my diary, which at that stage was a mixture of coded crush-confessions plus lists of daily activities that might just as well have been noted in advance.

Deep wedges of cupboard flanked the window. Dark and impenetrable, there was no way I could colonise these spaces and I hardly ever opened their doors. At the very front of the right-hand cupboard was a rail with some clothes. Not much to hang up: a grey skirt, a lime-green summer shift.

Between this cupboard and the fireplace was a wrought-iron, hand-painted, three-decker shoe-rack. It has taken me four sets of hyphenated phrases to describe it, which shows how ridiculous it was. It might have had a fascinating provenance, hence its retention in an upstairs nook such as my room, but I never heard that story. Nowadays you'd put it out in the garden or on a balcony and cover it with Busy Lizzies.

A gas fire was fitted into the narrow iron grate: ceramic flutes with Gruyère holes. The fire was as far from my bed as was possible. I had to jump out, turn on the brass tap, light the fire, dash back into bed, then slowly return to the weakly popping, faintly blue 'heat'. Ma used to sit by the fire when I was ill, fumy warmth mingling with the Dettol in a basin, soothing as any medicine.

I can't remember a mirror above the mantelpiece but I did brush my hair, long and unstyled as it was in those days. And I somehow drew dark mascara round my eyes Dusty Springfield-fashion and masked my lips with pale pink. At home the mirror was on the landing, communal. I saw myself at the turn of the stairs.

My room was papered with a pattern of flowers in faded pastels. I don't remember putting up any posters or other decorations on these walls. There was a carpet but I can't see it. In the centre of the floor was my wide plywood desk with a slanting lid painted royal blue. It came from our next-door neighbours when their daughter Suzette left home. They were half-French and had the first television in the street. I sat on their living-room rug to watch the Coronation in 1953.

21

I don't remember a mess on the floor of my room. Didn't I fling my clothes around? No junk food back then. And I never smoked. Dad's chain-smoking was enough. Did I have a laundry basket? Ma did all the washing, with her machine and her mangle and her flat irons, six shirts a day.

I sat in my room and looked out at my swaying tree. I relished the unsettling cupboards, the risky flat roof, the luminous radio and the potential for gatherings of friends away from the prying hordes downstairs. But there wasn't much stuff. You couldn't say that my room was full. Or that it was particularly age- or gender-related. More likely to be a bottle of ink than a bottle of nail varnish.

I didn't spend much time up there. It was cold, don't forget. Removed by three flights of stairs from all the gear Pearl had right there in her own room: television, telephone, record-player. Her room was a whole universe, filled with significant debris, sufficient for the life she wanted, precious, her active creation. Teenage rooms in the sixties were not complete in that way. And there wasn't much in my room that belonged to me. It was a vitrine of the fifties on hold, neither shut-off nor shut-in, not the centre of my adolescence but my space if I wanted it.

In the 1950s our outdoor spaces were the garden and the street but in the 1960s I dashed around London by bus. During the week it was a bassoon lesson in Highgate or swimming practice at the old baths on Finchley Road. On Saturdays it was the Biba-run, down to Kensington Church Street on the number 28 from Fortune Green. You could go in with your Marks & Spencer jumper and skirt and come out in velvet psychedelia, angular monochrome minis or granny's revival high-necked Viyella. For a couple of years Saturdays were highly ritualised. Mary and I and two school friends, also sisters, would take a 159 bus down Abbey Road and Lisson Grove to the Seymour Hall swimming baths, then a 31 bus across to Chalk Farm and Marine Ices, another 31 back over to Maida Vale for scrambled eggs at our friends' house, followed by Monopoly on a bedroom floor. There were variations depending on the season and whether or not someone had lent us roller-skates or even ice-skates. Then we might forego the swimming baths for Paddington Recreation Ground or Queen's Ice Rink in Bayswater. Our friends lived in a flat in Elgin Avenue. Their bikes were in the hallway. They were allowed to cycle to school, a hilly trek across Edgware Road, up through St John's Wood and along Finchley Road to Swiss Cottage.

In photographs from those years my mother stands to attention (like the soldier she had been) or folds a protective arm over her stomach (like the mother she was). Yet here she is in the West Hampstead garden, sitting on a wicker chair outside the sitting-room French windows. She is elegant in a moss green shift with a cardigan round her shoulders. Not looking at the camera. Pickle the Border terrier is standing on her lap, staring out to sea. That afternoon a friend of Anne's backcombed my first beehive.

Ma would pad round the house at night, her life-long patrol. Let's say it's now after eleven. 'Go to bed,' she pleads, just as she did from the beach on holiday, 'Come in!' from the undercurrents of the North Sea. Her voice isn't cold or cross, it's a loop: stop, lie down, rest, stay here. She didn't forbid me to go out, but I hardly ever did. Her anxieties were never spelled out but they suffused my teenage spaces. If we went out together it was different. She had great energy for theatre and shopping trips. We saw Maggie Smith in *The Master Builder*, Vanessa Redgrave in *As You Like It*. Those were the days when it was trendy for the Royal Shakespeare Company to play the

Ma with Pickle on her lap, 1963

still-compulsory national anthem (eighteenth century) on sackbuts (sixteenth). Later on we would meet for lunch at Cranks in Marshall Street, where she worked for the Family Planning Association clinic behind the swimming baths. She also worked at their clinic in North Kensington. All the FPA volunteers seemed to have at least five children themselves. Ma loved being with the women and children and I can't imagine her encouraging people to have fewer babies. Cranks was staffed by New Zealand women in sleeveless light-blue paisley dresses. They served us our very first quiche and salad.

Ma lingered in the kitchen after supper, elbows on the table, smoking a cigarette with her coffee, the smell of cottage pie or chops and vegetables fading in the fug. She did not ask us to clear away or do the washing up. She never expected us to help, much easier that way. If she'd insisted, there would be noise, fighting and breakages. The kitchen was large and dark, a few steps down from the hall, flat irons on the old black range, windows at the side and on to the garden. The only sign of modernisation was a yellow Formica worktop, made by Mr Smith-the-builder, opening up the original pantry and scullery. The white and navy enamel cooker and fridge stood on their short legs. A wooden dresser with glass doors and tall cupboards at either end was painted that post-war pale blue. There was always a stock of NHS orange juice and powdered milk. The cat and the dog slept companionably underneath. On Saturday mornings Irish Mary came to help. She put the chairs upside down on the table to wash the kitchen floor, her cigarette ash falling gently onto the clean tiles. Then Ma drove her home to Kilburn. Irish Mary was sweet, ageless. She had bottle-top glasses and dyed orange hair. She's there at my wedding, smart in a cream coat and red hat.

Ma liked to fill up the house. It was already full, of course. Aunty Spot lived with us in the mid-1950s, after working for the World Health Organization in Thailand. Tibor was an émigré from the Hungarian uprising in 1956, a doctor who came to us through Quaker doctor friends in Essex. He ate white bread with fatty bacon and spread Marmite on chocolate biscuits. There was Dr Kelsey, a friend of Aunty Spot's, who lived in the room that would later become mine. In the sixties my Indian school-friend Anu lived with us for two years to do O-levels after her parents returned to Delhi. Paul, John and Chris were student friends of Anne's, now in London to become actors and journalists. One summer it was rumoured that a whole swimming team was camped up there. In the fifties there were au pairs: Rosalie and Anne-Marie from Switzerland and Mantalena from Greece, who became so overexcited one bonfire night she ran around the garden with sheets of flaming newspaper and had to be taken to the police station in Fortune Green Road.

Sunday lunch was the only time we all sat down together in the dining room. During the week, my father would make his way to the sitting room when he came home from the office and stay there for the evening, worn out. We could go and eat with him or be with Ma in the kitchen, as we liked. Dad would come down to the kitchen for lunch on Saturdays. As in Eduardo de Filippo's play *Saturday, Sunday, Monday*, on Sundays there would be anticipation as the house filled with the smells of roast lamb and baked apples. Then, round the table erupted the rows and the rushing-out, followed, eventually, by a truce. My father had endless stamina for argument and jokes but if he was particularly irritated he would turn on the radio, handily within reach: Two-way Family Favourites, between British Forces Posted Overseas and their families at home, or Gardeners' Question Time. He couldn't care less about popular music or plants. You wouldn't know this from his rapt expression or the careful tapping of his right hand. Emailing is the new Sunday lunch. We can all speak at the same time, as we always did, but the soundlessness and time delay makes it easier to withstand corrections of fact or stabs of ridicule.

Suffolk
In the early sixties my parents bought a cottage in Suffolk, a few miles inland from Walberswick, where we had rented a cottage every

August for the previous decade. As usual, we were not told anything in advance. Westleton would give my father more scope for rides in his hand-propelled three-wheeler. That at least was true. There was only one way out of Walberswick by road, the switch-back slog along to the water tower at Blythburgh. From Westleton he would be able to go off in any direction. My parents were offered a house in Walberswick near the harbour but there were two major disadvantages: many flights of stairs and its proximity to the pub. It's clear from his correspondence with the estate agent that my father was looking ahead to his retirement in 1968, when he'd be sixty. Walberswick was too expensive anyway.

Now we had Holly Cottage we could go to Suffolk at New Year and Easter as well as in August. This was all good. But I spent the next couple of summers in angry denial of the move. Every day, Mary and I cycled across heath and forest back to our real village. It felt odd to be eating a packed lunch on the wartime pillbox

Family supper, Holly Cottage, 1963

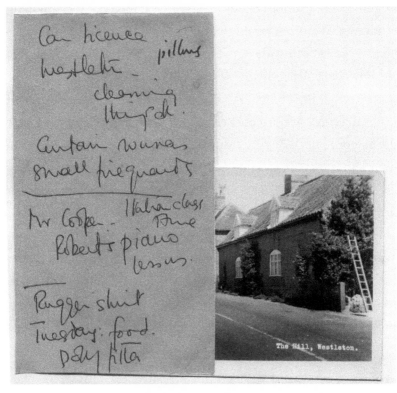

Ma's to do list / Holly Cottage

above the Walberswick marshes rather than in one of our rented houses nearby, especially as my mother's hardboiled eggs tended to slither down our trousers when we cracked their shells. But it was unthinkable not to be where my summer life of friends and freedoms awaited. The riding stables up a lane off the village street were my teenage hangout. Where I felt outside the family front door as well as out in the air. There was nowhere like that for me in London.

Westleton did gradually come to life. As a student I worked in The Crown as a waitress for the women who ran it: Ruth loud and rumpled, Winks stern and elegant. They were a double act of wonderful backstage cooking and front-of-house chic. I played music for hours with our next-door neighbours. I passed my driving test in Lowestoft. There was a boyfriend, too, for a while. He'd been to Antarctica with the Geological Survey and loved it. His snow-blindness back in crowded England never cleared.

School

The school gym was lined with wall-bars, windows high above. The jumping horse and the piano crowded together by the fire exit. Our 'shorts' consisted of yards of dark blue serge, heavy and scratchy, pleated, folded, hemmed and divided, reaching almost to our knees. Our aertex shirts were yolk-yellow. In the far corner stood a wooden gibbet and its metal accomplice. One by one we'd be taken, the bell would be no release from Weighing and Measuring. Teachers softened us up with a bad-cop, good-cop routine as we shuffled round the edge of the room, swallowing the urge to make a dash for the door. Every year I hoped the staff would shrug and sigh and wave away the last few letters of the alphabet, suddenly tired of it all, the cruel blue, black and red ink waiting to brand me with embarrassment.

At school, girls could be 'sporty', never 'fit'. *Keep Fit with Eileen Fowler* was TV drill for post-partum housewives tightening up to dance music in pastel leotards. There was no understanding that fitness could be for everyone whatever their bodies looked like. 'Gymnastics' was not taken seriously as a discipline. In the school's cultural confusion of ancient and modern there even lingered the award of 'posture girdles' alongside prizes for academic, artistic and sporting achievement. These were soft belts striped lengthways in the school colours of navy and gold, worn knotted at the hip like

29

a tie. A wearable Victorian relic. Given in front of the whole school in recognition of 'poise'.

The bell finally rang. In the gym my cheeks were clammy. 'Please let me go,' I silently pleaded. Yet I remember a kind of peace in the emptying room. I began to imagine getting out alive now that the shame of it was right there in front of me. The gibbet creaked as the teacher pushed on its stiff arm, up, up, up, a bit more, up. 'Stand up straight!' The scales giggled as I stepped onto the floating platform and brass balances were notched further into double figures. I was pinned down in their accounting books. The younger teacher smiled and put a hand on my shoulder, sisterly, 'till next year, then'.

My father made one visit to the school. Not to discuss my progress with the teachers but to give a talk. The Hall was dark, long windows not letting in much brightness despite our motto, Goethe's supposed last words: 'Mehr Licht' (More Light). The place was full, everyone standing as my father came slowly down to the platform from the swing doors at the back. I watched as he took his careful time. His approach was simpler than former American President Franklin Delano Roosevelt but they had a lot in common. FDR, disabled by polio when he was thirty-nine, would approach a stage as slowly and as upright as my father that afternoon. They looked alike too: square-headed, a jovial upper half, a pinched lower half, grimace held in check as they worked a crowd with their charm. But FDR had his son James at his elbow so he could dispense with one of his sticks. And it was known that he blacked out the joint of metal that went from his splints into his boot to prevent any flash of calliper steel. Dad threw each leg forward in turn, rolling on his heels, sticks planted firmly on the herringbone parquet: left, right, left, right. You couldn't tell from his shoulders how much effort this was. Like FDR my father 'walked' all the way. Like the President he was as supported as if he had ridden a wheelchair, which would have taken him to the front in no time. The imperative was not to be helped. Dad's slow pace was processional, fitting the ceremony.

He talked about newspapers. About the way they looked now, in the early sixties. More photographs than before, more papers set out horizontally, easier to read than columns of small print. He discussed how layout came to be associated with the different politics of each one. His tone was easy and friendly and interested. Perhaps he remembered the BBC Schools Broadcasting he had done in the war, how important it was to speak directly to youngsters. He had no script or illustrations, just his voice. He said, as he did to us at home: 'Read them for yourself.' My mother waited outside with the engine running, watching out for him but not helping when he picked his way down the concrete steps to the street.

A school friend recently downsized from her family home of the past thirty-five years. Sorting through the attic she found letters and postcards I sent to her in the sixties when I was away on holiday. I see that my style could be overblown like my father's and that I used words taken from both my parents' mouths: 'splendid' (my father) and 'frightful' (my mother). In one letter I tell my friend: 'I am reading a little fiction. I spend the day riding or swimming or just loafing and talking. Two hours becomes a mythical vacuum. However, I hope to read about 5 essential books (out of 25!)'. I tell her that my older sister Anne 'is back from Stratford at last and has seen the Beatles' film 3 times and says it's fantastic'. Another time I sent her a postcard because 'I've a million who've made me swear' to write to them as well. I share my passion for athletics: 'It's a marvellous thing to watch the Tokyo Olympics, except that that meeting got dreadful write-ups because of the 5,000 metres etc.' I remember that this was the first Olympic Games in Asia and the last with a cinder track, but I can't now remember what it was about the 5,000-metre race that upset reporters. In a letter I tell my friend about being my cousin Roy's bridesmaid up on the moors in County Durham. I enjoyed it, I liked the shiny lemon dress and felt important being chauffeured to Newcastle station to see Roy and Margaret off on honeymoon. Then I recap on end-of-term feelings: 'I managed abysmally', 'I came away feeling most unsettled'. And I tell her that 'Ma says I'm behaving nervily', like a 'screaming neurotic'.

Friends bunked off school to smoke pot at the Witches Cauldron in Belsize Village. I never joined them. The closest I got to truanting was the escape from Friday games, especially when it was hockey, in winter, in Regent's Park. All I had to do was claim severe period pains and repeat this at three rather than the expected four weeks. The teachers were far too shy to question me. Then it was off on a 13 bus down to the Academy cinema in Oxford Street. I saw the Russian *Hamlet* at least half a dozen times, snared by the language, the wild landscape and Shostakovich's score. I sent a fan letter to Innokenty Smoktunovsky. He sent me a signed photo. I was also seduced by the dissolving proscenium arch in *Les Enfants du Paradis*, shown at the Academy every year: the tinny fantasy of Les Funambules, the disturbing thrill of being inside Garance's head and heart, Jean-Louis Barrault's sad clown-hero, only tarnished by the question of his theatre company's performances in wartime Paris. These films were two-way projections and I was swept into their dreams and nightmares.

On teenage Friday afternoons there was ballroom dancing in the school hall. I had to be the man, foxtrotting backwards on the polished wooden floor. In the pleasure of the music and movement and despite the absence of actual men, this was one way I came to understand that what mattered beyond school was male approval. The dancing was Homage.

At university, young women enjoyed sex with whoever they chose. But mini-skirted liberation was curtailed by the old dependent values. Lecturers might be well known for their serial seduction of students, but if they didn't fancy you or me, the cry went up 'Why not?' They were never called out for abusing authority. The 50s and 60s overlaid each other in a very slow turning of the tide.

From our classroom confines, the fleshly conceits of the poetry of Donne and Marvell, the provocative wit of Congreve's play *The Way of The World* and the daring assertion of free spirits in E.M. Forster's novel *Howard's End* all stoked our theoretical belief in the rights of passion. Romantic fantasies of well-read teenagers would find themselves imprinted on those who moved across this limited landscape. The agonies of heightened feeling did hold a true sort of love. I poured my heartfelt self into this virginal, 50s-leftover space and ran about going nowhere. Nowhere near the confidence I would need all too soon.

Books and Curiosity

I arrived on Teesside a hundred years after the defining event of my father's life. In the early summer of 1911 his family went by train from North Yorkshire to Hampshire to stay with an uncle. They made the long trip in order to see the Review of the Fleet at Spithead on the Solent, a spectacle celebrating the Coronation of King George V. More than fifty years later my father told my brother Christopher that he had a memory of climbing out of his great-uncle's horse-drawn carriage by himself. This was the day before. His last day of being able to walk. The next day all he remembered was 'waking up on a couch'. He had contracted polio. He was three years old.

'I didn't get properly on my feet, with leg-irons or callipers to support me, until ten or a dozen years later.' He never told us the story. These words come from a talk he gave on BBC Radio's *Woman's*

Hour in 1959. We discovered the typescript after he died. In the talk, Donald praised his family, especially his mother, Catherine:

> My family were devoted but they were, I think, devoted in the right way. We were very poor in those days. Their every aim was to help me to help myself. I was lucky. Lucky above all in my mother, who was convinced that I would walk, even when everybody, including doctors as well as relatives and friends, said I never would.

Donald's wife Margaret used rather different language to confirm this view of Catherine:

> His mother was very, very determined. She was a hard Northerner but she was quite tough and she never helped him if he could do anything. She would say, 'Go along then', if he was crawling. I would have been much too soft-hearted. And, of course, they had no money, so she had to be tough.

A journalist colleague once asked my father if he could remember being able to walk. 'I remember climbing over a gate,' he replied. 'Yes,' added my mother, 'there's a photograph by this same gate, a little fair-haired boy at home with his grandmother in Yorkshire.' Only one photograph of my father before he had polio. I stop to think about this. As far as I was concerned my father had always been unable to walk. Now I became properly aware that this wasn't true. He'd had more than a year of walking.

Half a century before vaccination against polio became widely available in Britain, Donald endured prolonged and painful treatment. 'I've been what the doctors called "an old polio",' he told his *Woman's Hour* audience. The specific virus was identified around the time my father became ill. Before then the condition was simply called 'infantile paralysis'. He spent long periods in Middlesbrough's West Lane Fever Hospital, where, my mother said, 'the men played cards with him and he was taught to read and that was his education.'

The only books in the hospital were the twenty-nine volumes of the brand-new Eleventh Edition of the Encyclopaedia Britannica, volumes 1–14 appearing in 1910 and the rest in 1911, published jointly by Cambridge University Press and Horace Everett Hooper, as it transferred from British to American ownership. Hugh Chisholm was editor-in-chief. The volumes appeared together as an unprecedented continuous run, making cross-references possible for the first time. There were more than 40,000 articles, some of them ten times longer than those in earlier editions. Ernest Barker's entry on the Crusades in volume 7 extends over twenty-nine double-columned pages. I read that Joseph Vaughan discovered ironstone in the Easton hills of North Yorkshire in 1851. There is no entry for 'polio'.

It was a gigantic collaboration. Edmund Gosse, author of *Father and Son* and Librarian of the House of Lords, was the chief literary editor. Contributors included Matthew Arnold, Major Baden-Powell, Gertrude Bell, Walter Crane, Thomas Huxley, Alice Meynell, William Morris, Lord Macaulay, Lord Northcliffe, Arthur Quiller-Couch, William Michael Rossetti, Leslie Stephen, RL Stevenson and Algernon Swinburne. The Index, compiled by Janet Hogarth with the help of Miss Griffiths, Miss Tyler and Miss Edmonds, took up the whole of volume 29. A full list of contributors came at the end: William Napier Shaw, MA LLD D Sc. FRS, wrote on 'Dew. Fog.

Squall. Sunshine', Professor Henry Preserved Smith wrote on 'Papal history', Thomas Whitridge on 'Animal worship. Cannibalism. Clairvoyance. Divination, Dreams. Fetishism', and Surgeon-Major George Dobson on 'Mole (in part). Shrew. Vampire'. Even reading the index is fun.

The University Extension movement began in Cambridge in 1871 to promote the university as a national institution 'for the general diffusion of knowledge and culture'. Their local examinations gave the university contact with the new secondary education and the encyclopaedia would provide 'a thorough elucidation of important scientific problems for which the modern enquirer has no adequate textbooks'. This edition aimed 'at achieving the high ambition of bringing all extant knowledge within the reach of every class of reader'. I can see Donald, a small boy sitting up in his hospital bed, or propped up on a chair, grasping one of those enormous books, fascinated by every topic, learning to read, storing his memory.

The life of paralysed youngsters was isolated and confined. Plaster casts kept limbs straight. When these were too tight it was agony. Muscles withered unnecessarily. There was no physiotherapy. One young girl, Mary, born in Newcastle a year before Donald, also contracted polio when she was three. She did not go to school till she was ten. She was systematically stripped of her gender. As a fever patient, her hair was cut off to conserve energy, and because she was massaged every day with olive oil her white nighties became 'browny-grey'. She had a navy-blue boy's jersey to wear on top. The doctors would call her 'my little man'. She felt she'd been turned into a non-person. I read her story in a collection of the childhood reminiscences of people with disabilities and she came back into my mind when I was thinking about Donald's brief year of running about. A brief year of walking and running about before a decade or more of total immobility. Total dependence for a dozen years of his childhood. Mary's steel callipers and corset were made by Mr Ernst, an elderly German she visited several times a year to have alterations made as she grew. About the time his father died, Donald was referred to a splint-maker whose shop was at Sillis Strudwick, Albert Street, Camden Town but who lived in a cottage on the Hatfield estate in Hertfordshire, where his wife was a servant in the royal household. So it happened one day, as Donald was wheeled round the gardens of Hatfield House, he was kissed by Queen Alexandra.

Donald had gone to stay in Hatfield because the splints were made to measure by hand. The craftsman was passionate about cricket and taught Donald to bat and bowl. Walking with his sticks and splints gave Donald strong arms, very useful for a cricketer. The splint-maker also taught Donald how to fall properly. An essential skill during the wartime blackout in Fleet Street twenty years later, though it could also be dramatically misinterpreted, as I discovered in my teens.

The places of my father's early life have often been renamed: North Yorkshire – Teesside – Cleveland – Middlesbrough. County Durham – Tyne and Wear – Gateshead. Donald Tyerman would later say he was all in favour of change. As a child, he had no choice. Instability was his daily experience.

I did not know any of my grandparents. Both grandfathers died in their early forties, the span of their lives from the late 1870s to the early 1920s. It is hard to feel they were related to my parents, let alone to me. Donald's maternal grandparents were William Day, a builder and ironmonger from Guisborough, North Yorkshire, and his wife, Anne Bargate. Donald's mother, Catherine Day, was born in Dundee in 1879. Donald's father, Joseph Tyerman, was also born in 1879, in the Foundry House, Easington, home of his parents Joseph and Hannah Tyerman. Middlesbrough had grown fast after the discovery of iron ore in the mid-nineteenth century. Streets were laid out on a grid system, spreading quickly on the south bank of the Tees. My grandfather Joseph was living at 132 Victoria Road, Middlesbrough before he married Catherine in 1901.

The Tyermans were by tradition Methodist. John Wesley visited North Yorkshire during the wintry April of 1745. Late on the night of the 15th and early the following morning, he preached at Osmotherley. There he baptised a baby girl called Elizabeth Tyerman. One of my grandfather's sisters was Elizabeth Tyerman. My younger brother's daughter is Elizabeth Tyerman. Her brother, Edward, is also named Joseph after his great- and his great-great grandfather. In the mid-nineteenth century, Methodist historian Luke Tyerman wrote biographies of the Wesleys, father John and his sons John and Charles.

Census returns show that the name Tyerman belongs to the North East, particularly County Durham and North Yorkshire. There's a Tyerman Passage in Whitby. In *The Lodger*, a tantalising glimpse into Shakespeare's life in London, Charles Nicholl presents a lively possible origin of the name. 'Head-tires come in many shapes and sizes,' he tells us. 'The word "tire" – then also written "tyre", "tier" and "tyer" – is simply an abbreviated form of "attire".' While this implies the domestic servant who helps you dress, a valet or maid, the image of 'Tyremen' and 'tyrewomen' making headgear for fashionable ladies and actors in Shakespeare's London is far more attractive.

My grandfather Joseph described himself, at different times, as a moulder, a coal merchant, a cashier and a solicitor's accountant.

He was the handsome chancer, literate and good with numbers, quick-witted, brashly going off towards the next big thing, at home or abroad, leaving his wife and children for unpredictable periods of time. My mother heard he had 'immense charm and was totally improvident'. My cousin Roy describes our Tyerman grandparents' relationship as on-off, on-off. He was in his late teens when Catherine died:

> Grandma Tyerman as I knew her was certainly very strong-willed, resilient, with a volatile temper. However, she was also very kind and caring. When she was teaching at the toughest of schools in Gateshead, Windmill Hills School, she used to get shoes for the poorest of the children. Many were in their bare feet in those days. Her discipline was also strong. The mothers of the children called her the 'bob-tailed bitch'. During a very nomadic existence she had numerous homes and never seemed to settle for long but she quickly made any new abode feel like home. She was a great reader and encouraged me. She gave me *Lark Rise to Candleford* when I was about twelve. She was an accomplished cook who took great pride in her Yorkshire puddings and the beautiful gravy she made to accompany them.

My grandparents' personalities, his chancer-confident, hers anxious but determined, are clearly illustrated in their handwriting. I found Joseph's inside an American thriller and Catherine's on the flyleaf of a novel by Francis Brett Young. His script is bold and swirly, the capital letters swinging up and down and out to the side, a sloping line flourishing across the page underneath. Hers is small and neat, instantly legible – and instantly familiar. Catherine's writing is exactly like my father's.

Donald was the second of Joseph and Catherine's three sons. A formal photograph, taken in 1920, shows Donald, aged twelve, standing on the left, Reg, six years older, sitting on a stool in the middle, and Harry, four years younger, standing on the right. Perhaps it was taken after their father died, to mark family mourning. Life would be a lot more settled for the brothers. And I see that Donald holds a stick in his right hand, splints bracing each leg. He is standing on his own, for the first time since the Hampshire holiday. The brothers are close. There's a dynamic to their stillness. Almost a century later, Donald's firm stare at the camera has lost none of its power.

Reg was born in 1902 at Routledge House, a semi-detached villa in Limes Road, Linthorpe, the home of his paternal grandparents in a newly developed district south of Middlesbrough. Doreen was born in there in 1905 but died in 1907. Donald was born there the following year. His birthday was 1 March. Officially. Perhaps he was born before midnight, on 29 February, leap year day and to be avoided. From 1909 the young family lived for a few years at Cliff Rigg House, West Terrace, Great Ayton, the home of Catherine's parents. Harry was born there in 1912 and Mary in 1913. This is the place of Donald's earliest memories. The place we see in that photograph of the fair-haired young boy standing with his grandmother.

After another two years back in Middlesbrough and a brief return to Great Ayton, between 1917 and 1918 Donald was with his mother, father and brother Harry in Mombasa, Kenya. Donald's father twice went off by himself to Africa. From 1913–15 Joseph worked for Cadbury's in Takoradi on the Gold Coast in British West Africa. From 1917–18 he was in Kenya. This time, uninvited,

Donald, Reg and Harry, 1920

Catherine took her three younger children out to join him. Four-year-old Mary died on the voyage. Fifteen-year-old Reg stayed behind with friends in Great Ayton.

I open the album of photographs and postcards from Kenya. There's even a picture of the family with a snake charmer, blanched figures on a latticed verandah. One boy is sitting on a bentwood chair, dressed in white but his shoes and leggings are black. The couple standing behind him are my grandparents, Joseph and Catherine Tyerman, dark-eyed and strong-jawed. The child on the bentwood chair is Donald. The child standing on the right is his younger brother Harry. The little boys look bewildered, like wilting cherubs. At the centre of the picture is the Indian, sitting knees up on a mat, keeping himself and the snake still for the exposure. At his feet lie the paraphernalia of his act but I can't see the pipe he would need for the mesmerising. In his right hand he grips the snake's jerking head. I don't know who compiled the album. Catherine had not been expected, after all, and the journey had been fatal to Mary. Joseph may well have been running away, from the war, as well as from his family, which he did from time to time, chasing work, hoping for a respite, leaving them in rented rooms or lodging with in-laws. Who would want to remember? The whole image looks forced and stiff, all of them trapped in the amber of Imperial fantasy.

When Catherine and the children came home from Kenya they did not return to North Yorkshire but moved up to Gateshead, County Durham. Reg was going to study mining engineering at Armstrong College in Newcastle (later Newcastle University but then part of Durham University). Reg was in his second year of his course when his father came back from Africa. Joseph caught pneumonia soon afterwards and died in the bungalow in Church Road, Low Fell,

Donald standing, North Yorkshire, 1910

Donald sitting, Kenya, 1915

on 12 January 1921. The house was down a long flight of steps from the road and Reg remembered how difficult it was to carry down the oxygen cylinders for his father, especially in the snow.

Donald's childhood was exceptionally unstable. The list of his childhood homes is long, the list of schools not much shorter. Between 1909 and 1918, after the seven years in his paternal grandparents' house in Middlesbrough and before the eight years in Gateshead, there were five moves, including the African episode. Donald attended four different schools in the North East: a Quaker school, a Roman Catholic College, an Anglican boarding school and a Municipal Secondary School. The moves reflect Joseph and Catherine's fluctuating finances and unstable relationship. First, Donald attended The Friends' School in Great Ayton as a 'day scholar' from September 1915 to April 1917, aged seven to nine. Donald's brothers, Reg and Harry, also attended the school, as, later, did his nephew Roy. Quakers had been in the North East of England since the 1650s and at Great Ayton since 1700. Members of the Fry family, Quakers famous for chocolate-making, are buried in the graveyard. The school closed in the 1990s and is now housing. The conservation of the old and the building of new houses was carried out by Wimpey, the company that built the White City stadium for the London Olympic Games of 1908, the year of Donald's birth.

In the autumn of 1915, Donald was placed sixth in his class at the Quaker school, in the following spring, second, and by the summer of 1916, first. The next year was not so good. He was ill, his father was away, his brother Reg was also ill during this time and his paternal grandfather was dying. At the General Meeting Day on 15 July 1950, Donald, then Deputy Editor of *The Times*, gave the address to the school community, known as 'The Family'. His mother, Catherine, his brother Reg, and nephew Roy, then Head Boy, were in the audience. *The Real Community* was published as a supplement to the school magazine, *The Beckside*, named because the village is on a river, the Leven:

> We lived in lots of places through the years, but somehow Ayton kept a special place all the time in all our minds and all our hearts. When we have thought of Home, this village had always been remembered. When we have spoken of School, this

46

school has come first to mind. You have here in this school a *Community* [Donald's italics], a real community, a living community. That's a rare thing and a precious thing in these days of artificial living, of broken ties and broken bonds, of rush and haste and anxiety and fear, of short sightedness and material goals.

My father reflects on the legacy he's passing on to his three young daughters:

I remember spending at least one night – I was a day boy – in the Headmaster's, Mr. Dennis's, house. Here the explanation of Reg is wrong. Reg says this pleasant, brief exile, was probably due to my mother's inability to cope with my wild rages at home. To the rages I sadly confess; my small daughters have them now, which is Nemesis indeed. But I'm pretty sure that I was boarded out in this dignified fashion on this occasion because Reg himself was seriously ill.

Here it was that Donald 'first saw and first read *Uncle Remus* and *Brer Rabbit*'. And in Miss Arnold's classroom, as very young boy, Donald had a crucial epiphany:

I can say that here in the classroom by the rushing water I got my first compass bearing on what to do in life, though lame, my first sense that independence is the way, that *my way* was by books and curiosity, that I could still be an individual in the community. It was Miss Arnold who gave me these things, things that have seen me through.

47

After the year in Kenya without any schooling, Donald, aged ten–twelve, became a day boy at St Mary's Roman Catholic College in Middlesbrough. He did well but in 1920 Catherine moved him to a boarding school. In a letter to her, headmaster Rector James Moran wrote: 'We shall be sorry to lose him.' From September 1920 to July 1921 Donald boarded at Sir William Turner's Anglican School in Redcar. Yet another short stay. When he left Donald was awarded the Everyman edition of *The Diary of Samuel Pepys* as a first prize 'For General Excellence' and in Donald's report for the summer of 1921, headmaster Reverend D.N. Littler wrote: 'We are sorry to lose him.'

In September 1921 Donald went to Gateshead Municipal Secondary School:

> The only school to which I really belonged, the one to which I really owe what schooling I have, whose masters and mistresses gave me, by their skill and devotion, my start in life. The school, where I spent some years not just a few terms, was the most ordinary perhaps of them all.

I have his dark green School Report Book. The white label on the cover says: 'Gateshead Education Committee, Municipal Secondary School, Headmaster W. Walton, B.A'. Reading Catherine's signature at the bottom of each report reminded me of Donald's mother's central importance as his sole parent and guardian. In his first two years, Donald's form teachers were women: Miss Grey and Miss Derrick. From the summer of 1923 his teacher was William Miller, whose subject was maths. It was here that Donald was introduced to Gilbert and Sullivan operettas, performed regularly in the school. In the late 1950s he took us to the 'G&S' performances of the D'Oyly

Carte company at the Savoy Theatre in the Strand for a Boxing Day treat when we'd outgrown pantos at the Golders Green Hippodrome.

Donald was placed first in his class throughout his five years at the school, despite absences early in 1922 due to illness and the death of his father. In his final years Donald studied History, English, Latin and French. In 1922 and 1923 he was joint editor of the school magazine, though his composition could still be 'somewhat ponderous'. By 1925 his work in English was 'excellent'. At Christmas 1922, 'Needlework' was crossed out and replaced by 'Phys.Training', with the comment: 'Paralysis. Legs. Excused'. Similarly, at Easter: 'Phys.Training. Excused (Paralysis) Legs'. But by the summer of 1923, the comment was evolving: 'Excused (keen interest in sport)' and two years later Donald was described as an 'Excellent sportsman' with a 'keen interest in sports and games'. Sport would remain a lifelong passion. At school, Donald used to bowl and bat, a teammate standing by to run.

One friend from schooldays who shared this passion was Warbey Knight, a trainee teacher who later became Chief Education Office for Harrow County in North West London. The Knights then lived in Heronsgate, Chorleywood, an estate founded in the mid-1840s by the Chartist Cooperative Land Company to resettle urban workers with the aim of making them eligible for the vote. The Knights were one of the few families who would invite all seven of us, plus dog, to a weekend lunch. When my father died in 1981 Warbey wrote to my mother:

> Although Don's life embraced so many interests, causes and people, to Gwen and me it is the personal loss which affects us most deeply. All those of us who knew him in his Gateshead

days look back with pride on his achievements and are grateful for his friendship. Memories flood back – cricket on the little school playing field, canvassing along Church Road for the 1924 election, debates in the school hall, the cheerful badinage of the Sheriff Hill group as we walked to the tram. His has indeed been a worthwhile life, which has enriched the wider life of this country.

In 1925 Donald sat the Scholarship examinations at Oxford. He went through the alphabetical list of colleges to make his choice. Balliol College he judged too upper class. Brasenose College (BNC) came next. He won the Junior Hulme Scholarship, £100 a year for four years. He stayed on at school (what else could he do?) and took more Higher Certificate exams in July 1926 to add to those he took the previous summer. 'OXFORD SCHOLARSHIP', was the headline in the local press. 'Gateshead Student's Fine Achievement'. Advertised on the reverse page are 'Tilleys' Saturday Dances in the Grand Assembly Rooms, Barras Bridge. Tea-Dance 3–6pm at 2/6, After Dinner Dance 6–11.45pm, at 5/-'. The article describes Donald as a 'cripple' but says he 'took his place in the school cricket team' and was regarded as a 'thorough sport'. When Donald was appointed Editor of the *Economist* in 1955, 'GATESHEAD BRILLIANCE' was the local headline. Donald was 'Probably Gateshead Secondary School's most brilliant pupil'.

It was cold when I visited Middlesbrough, seagulls circling with sore-throated cries. Between the old Town Hall and MIMA, the city's new art gallery, designed by Dutch architect Erick van Egeraat, patterned ironwork is set into the grass commemorating the local industry. Alongside this regeneration I came across a derelict 1960s office block of glass, metal and concrete called Permanent House. To the south, Albert Park has become an Asian neighbourhood. On the day of my walk men and boys were playing cricket on a green at the end of Newstead Road, a sight Donald would have relished, for the sport and for the family connection. His mother Catherine died in 1951. She lived in Newstead Road for the last seven years of her life.

My mother was born Margaret Gray in Wallington, South London in 1912, the youngest of three sisters. Jessie was born in 1906 and 'Spot' in 1908. Spot because she was small, a 'spot of love'. Her first name was Florence but friends and colleagues called her Leslie, her middle name and mine. Their mother, Ida, was only forty when her husband Ernest died of pneumonia in 1920, aged forty-one. He always had problems with his lungs. Though a trained nurse and now a widow with three young daughters, Ida would not take any paid work. Such were the conventions of respectability. 'It was a dreadful time,' my mother later wrote, 'genteel poverty is an awful blight'. Ida died in 1937, in her late fifties, 'thus being spared the trauma of the war'.

Margaret remembered her early childhood on the Downs above Brighton as 'an idyllic time'. She rode on her father's shoulders. He made enchanting drawings of their cats. There was singing round the piano. After he died it was so different. 'My mother regarded her family, especially me, the youngest, as a burden which had spoiled her life.' Hers had been a difficult birth, though Margaret was never told what had happened. She was always taller and more substantial than her sisters. You could see her fear of blame in her posture: hesitant, bending in the middle, holding her arms across

51

Catherine and Joseph Tyerman, Ida and Ernest Gray

her stomach, smiling wanly or looking at a camera with a direct but uncertain gaze.

At home there was bottled-up frustration followed by 'explosions behind closed doors', the everlasting battles between Ida and Jessie, both grieving but unable to share it. When there was screaming and shouting at home, Spot would take Margaret out for long walks. When there was screaming and shouting at home during my own childhood, my mother was the first to leave the room.

Ida's behaviour was 'odd'. When Margaret's sister Leslie, now working as a health visitor, had committed some small misdemeanour in her mother's eyes, Ida telephoned the clinic and told them to tell Leslie that her father had died. He had been dead for twelve years. On another occasion Ida sent a telegram to Margaret, away at college, saying, 'Come home at once'. When Margaret arrived, Ida said, 'Now you are here, you can do the washing up.' Two cups and one plate.

My mother said she felt 'disloyal' writing about it all sixty years on, but also 'pity'. She described her mother as 'intelligent, energetic, attractive, frustrated'. She was describing herself too. Ida was a victim of her times, a pre-welfare state widow with no benefits or free health care but hidebound by class expectations from earning a living. Downward mobility was a disgrace and Margaret understood her mother's lack of freedom.

When Margaret was in her early teens they moved from Brighton to Clapham in South London, renting a flat at 136 Rodenhurst Road, a street of late Victorian and Edwardian villas to the south of the Common. 'It was strange and lonely at first,' she wrote. Her oldest sister, Jessie, who was by then working in the City, now had a much easier commute but she was also disturbed by the move. Her adult social life was completely interrupted. Like Margaret, Jessie lacked confidence and found the adjustment hard. Her relationship with her sister was complex: intrusive and carping but also generous. In later years Jessie would give my mother clothes, furniture or kitchen equipment, she would invite me to stay in the holidays and she supported us financially. But she was also critical and jealous. Aunty Spot was Margaret's life-long confidante.

Margaret went to Clapham High School, her fees paid for by an uncle about whom I know nothing except that he was not willing to pay for Ida's younger girls, Leslie and Margaret, to go on to university. The family could not therefore afford the time or money needed for Margaret to apply, as had been expected, to Oxford or Cambridge. She went straight from school to Southampton University, then an external college of London University, which she said the school patronised as a 'very down market Teacher Training College'.

Ida had one quality that Margaret did appreciate at the time. She made sure her daughter would be able to continue her education. Ida appealed to the London County Council and managed to secure a grant, which was conditional on Margaret becoming a teacher after graduation. Ida also found a charitable trust whose criteria included the education of girls and the support of poor widows: the Thomas Wall Trust. My mother went to university on a grant from Wall's sausages.

My Northern grandparents lived in the homes of parents-in-law or rented rooms, in semi-detached houses with front gardens. They were intelligent but under-educated, enterprising but socially and financially insecure. Family life was so disrupted that it has been hard to work out exactly where my father was living when he

Margaret, her mother Ida, a neighbour and sister Jessie,
Clapham, late 1920s

attended which school, how often he was unwell and for how long,
when exactly he travelled south for treatment and the making of
his sticks and splints. Donald's life was much more stable after his
father died.

The roots of Donald's lifelong interests are clear: editing
the school magazine, a passion for sport, the Methodist/Quaker-
inspired commitment to social justice. Growing up in the depressed
North East would later fuel a nostalgia-free dedication to post-war
reconstruction. Donald was already a compulsive reader and talker.
Polio was an impetus as well as an impediment. Donald used to
say that but for polio he would have been a clerk on the LNER
railway. He described himself as 'lucky'. His immobility drove
the extremes of his personality: his 'wild rages' and his absolute

concentration. He described himself as 'lame'. I never heard him say he was 'disabled'.

My mother, Margaret, and my grandmother, Catherine, were both born in difficult circumstances and bore the weight of their own mothers' frustration and blame. There was no empathy between them and they never trusted each other. If they had been friends I would have known Catherine. Donald had to bear the conflict between his mother and his wife. My father never said a word against his mother. My mother could be bitter about her own. My father gritted his teeth against any slurs on his background. My mother said her early childhood had been 'idyllic'. As an impoverished widow, Catherine got on with it. My maternal grandmother, Ida, another impoverished widow, did not. Yet both women pushed hard for the education of their children.

I did not grow up in the landscapes of my parents and they did not tell their stories. I still feel as if my parents sprang from nowhere. Yet I also feel some connection to that generation I never knew, particularly the Tyermans of North Yorkshire and County Durham. I hear their voices in the Geordie accent of my cousin and his family.

My parents did not display images of themselves or their parents and there was only one formal set of photographs of us children, taken around 1960. There is a box of family photos, however, so we can look at the pictures they did not care to, retrieving our unknown grandparents after the deaths of their children. We can reproduce the images easily these days, too, and put them up in our own homes and look back as much as we like at where we came from.

Donald and Margaret wanted to start again.

Olympic Adventure

Twelve feet up in the air a car hangs suspended above the Calais dockside. A Morris 8, registration OW 8649. Long chains hang taut from a square metal frame and wrap round each wheel, ends dangling below. Dockers in dark shirts and berets take no notice of what strikes me as surreal and hilarious. In a photograph as big as my fingernail a great lump of metal is flying. The car arrived at the French port on the 11am ferry from Dover on Sunday, 30 July. Margaret, aged twenty-four, was about to drive Donald, twenty-eight, across Europe to the 1936 Berlin Olympic Games. They had known each other for six years and been married for two.

Donald came South in the autumn of 1926, from Gateshead Municipal Secondary School to the University of Oxford. It was a huge journey. The General Strike in May lasted only ten days but the Durham Miners' Lockout lasted till the end of the year. Donald never returned to live or work in the North East but it remained the backdrop to his life. Margaret's first visit was a shock:

> He'd been brought up in the North. I'd been brought up in the South in the very sort of conservative way. I remember the first time I went North to visit his family. We drove through that place where there was all this unemployment. It was a total emotional shock to me. There were men sitting on their haunches all along the street. They were out of work. I've never forgotten this awful picture. And he came from the North where people were starving. They were literally starving. There was no question of them putting coals in the bath and all that rubbish.

At Oxford Donald shared rooms overlooking the High Street. The nearest lavatory was across two quadrangles, quite an effort with his sticks and splints. He worked hard too. More than fifty years later, his American college roommate Andrew Berding wrote to my mother from Washington: 'Don was an inspiration and guiding light of my Oxford days. His courage, determination and brilliance were an invaluable impetus'. The only serious distraction was chess, which Donald learned at school and now played for his college. It could easily have taken over. He chose history over chess. In 1929 he gained a first class degree, doubly exceptional because Brasenose College was then known more for its sportsmen than for its scholars. Donald celebrated with champagne and fish and chips. He treated himself to performances of Gilbert and Sullivan's *Ruddigore* and Oliver Goldsmith's *She Stoops to Conquer* at the New Theatre. And some light reading in the Bodleian Library: *Buster* and *The Magnet*, the magazines of his youth.

Car in chains at Calais, August 1936

Donald began postgraduate research on the relation between industry and the banks in times of recession. This was how he honoured his upbringing. Like Matthew Price, the central character in Raymond Williams's *Border Country,* who took just as significant a journey a decade later than Donald, from a Welsh hamlet to Cambridge University, and also did not return. Matthew's life-long work was the sociology of the communities he left behind.

But Donald's four-year scholarship money ran out in 1930 and he had to get a job. He had no private funds, which was unusual for a junior academic at Oxford in those days. He was appointed Assistant Lecturer in Economic History at University College, Southampton. References came from Oxford and Gateshead. Headmaster Walton confirmed that Mr D. Tyerman was one of the school's 'most distinguished old pupils', with a 'fine personality, presence and address', who 'is not in any way handicapped by the physical infirmity from which he suffers'. C.H. Sampson, Principal of Brasenose College, wrote that 'Mr Donald Tyerman, B.A., and Senior Hulme Scholar of the College, is a man of sterling character and exceptional ability. I can speak from personal knowledge of the high regard in which he is held by all. He has the faculty of forming deep and lasting friendships. His strong sincerity of character may enable him to triumph over physical discouragements.' On 21 November 1930 Donald took out an endowment assurance policy with Scottish Widows Fund and Life Assurance Society, for a premium of £37 and 10 shillings, with £1,459, plus profits, payable in October 1967. This turned out to be more necessary than he could have imagined.

Donald and Margaret both arrived in Southampton in the autumn of 1930. Between Southampton and the Isle of Wight lies the Solent, the setting for that Naval Review of 1911. So for Donald, it was a return. He must have been reminded of that fateful holiday twenty years ago. For Margaret it was not that far along the coast westwards from her early childhood in Brighton. Donald was her tutor. The small university college was in Highfield, some way above the international port. The university's Principal from 1922 to 1946 was Kenneth Vickers. He also came from the North East and had been a Professor of History at Newcastle University. He was a keen cricketer, too. And he had had polio. Born in 1881 he belonged to the generation of Donald's parents. In that modest academic community, Professor Vickers was a father figure for Donald, a young man in his first job. When Donald moved to *The Times* in 1944 and wrote to tell him, Professor Vickers was delighted. 'I am quite certain that you have the ability to make good on this job and so I shall look forward to seeing you assistant Editor before very long and perhaps I shall live long enough to see you Editor. I hope so. You have had a hard row to hoe and you have hoed it very well.'

I've been carrying two letters around in my rucksack for ages, nearly reading them. There's one from Donald to Margaret and one from her to him. His letter is in a flimsy brown envelope, her envelope is stiff and cream-coloured. His handwriting is neat and clear and his letter covers one side of university headed notepaper. Her handwriting is large and vigorous, covering four ruled sheets of Basildon Bond. Donald's letter is undated but was written at least a year before their wedding. I can tell this because at the top he added: 'I lectured on the Agrarian Revolution. I missed you hellishly'. She was absent from her undergraduate lecture due to illness and he writes in response to a note from her. Margaret graduated in the summer of 1933 but they did not marry till she had completed the postgraduate teacher-training course that was a condition of her grant. Donald's letter has no postmark; it was sent 'by Mercury, if I can find him' across the Southampton University campus to Margaret's student residence. Her letter is postmarked '1 AUG 1935', a year after they got married.

Donald's letter is full of warm concern. He bets she's not feeling as well as she claims in her own letter excusing her absence. He writes in whole paragraphs but he's happily explicit: 'I love everything about you'. He says he loves her more than yesterday and less than tomorrow. He's also rather formal. He lists with an a) and a b) the arrangements he's made to meet friends for tea on a couple of occasions and asks her 'Is that alright?' He wants to show her off. He's aware he may sound foolish when he says he's longing to see her again, but, as he says, 'it's really very, very wise'.

Margaret's letter is funny in a black sort of way. She's on holiday with her mother in Scotland. Her letter is angry but resigned, full of wit at her inevitable failure to please Ida, referred to as 'M', who can't resist bragging, which Margaret can't bear. Ida offers her daughter's services as a driver to impress the owners of the guest house. Margaret goes off by herself to admire the view when she can. Her letter begins: 'I must write what I'm thinking – there's no one to hear my comments'. The owners are 'so blasted ladylike', simpering that they only take in guests 'to keep on the old home'. There was 'heaps more in that strain which M laps up'. Margaret says she actually quite likes the owners but hates the posing, 'be-damned say I'. She says 'I'm sorry darling – don't think I'm not happy, not enjoying it – but I must comment, as you know'. And she loves the house: 'square, on a hill, with a wonderful view of hills and river'. M likes it, too, so at least Margaret has got something right. She says: 'I love you and want to kiss you good night. I bet we have cold ham for supper!' She's returning to Southampton the following day, 'very excited about tomorrow – evening. All my love. Margaret.'

For Christmas 1933, Donald gave Margaret a copy of Vera Brittain's *Testament of Youth*. First published that summer in London by Victor Gollancz, the book was printed by the Camelot Press in Southampton. Donald inscribes the flyleaf: 'A prelude to Christmas 1933, with a sure hope of lasting youth and happiness – a testament of the future'. Underneath he writes 'M / Dec.1933 / D'.

They married on 30 June 1934. There were vociferous objections from Margaret's family. 'How can Baby marry this cripple!' cried Jessie, her oldest sister. Margaret herself later told us: 'My mother had allowed herself to relax. But then at the end of my time at Southampton I decided to get married. I think my mother had built up an unrealistic picture of me getting a job and caring for her from then onwards. Once more I felt I had let her down. But the turmoil was such that she was bound to lose. My husband-to-be had polio and was lame and this caused terrible trouble. She even tried to make her GP get it stopped.'

Donald and Margaret's wedding day turned into Germany's 'Night of the Long Knives'. Donald and Margaret spent their honeymoon in the ancient university town of Heidelberg. They stayed at the Schwarzes Schiff Hotel on Bergstrasse. They were having breakfast in a café towards the end of their holiday when radio broadcasting was interrupted by repeated singing of the 'Horst Wessel Lied' (Horst Wessel's Song), a song written by Wessel and adopted by the Nazi Party as an anthem after the Berlin stormtrooper's murder by communists in 1930 at the age of twenty-three. This eventually

Wedding, June 30th 1934

faded to make way for the hammer-blow voice of Hitler. Donald and Margaret listened and were shocked, glad to be going home soon. Witnessing this sign of horrors to come dispelled their commitment to peace. Nevertheless, they returned to Germany in 1936, as did Britons of all political persuasions.

I have a photograph of them back in England, sitting on a low garden wall, smiling. Behind the garden is a two-storey brick terrace. A flat arch curves over the downstairs windows with their rows of small panes. The central doorway has a Georgian porch. I had never seen the photo till my older sister Anne made copies for us not long ago and then I had no idea where it was taken. But I saw that Margaret had addressed her lovely letter to Donald at 2, Highfield Close (he kept the envelope) and when I visited Southampton I went to Highfield Close and there it was, the backdrop to the photograph. Number 2 is on the ground floor, a flat for a young married couple, accessible for Donald. He ordered a desk, three bookcases and a chest to be made by local furnishers Shepherd and Hedger.

Architectural historian Nikolaus Pevsner describes Highfield as 'the best piece of suburbia in Southampton', built 'in the finest garden city traditions'. In his essay 'Terminus City', Southampton native Owen Hatherley describes the area as a 'little Letchworth in the northern suburbs'. It was designed between 1920 and 1939 by Quaker architect Herbert Collins, who was also a member of the Welwyn Garden City Company. Living in their rented flat in Highfield added personal experience to the arguments for decent public housing Donald would make during and after the war.

A heat wave spread across Europe during the summer of 1936, accompanied by what Goronwy Rees, editor of *The Spectator*, remembered as the 'increasing shadow of politics'. In March the Germans occupied the Rhineland, in July the Spanish Civil War began. In Britain, the year started with the death of George V and ended with the Abdication of Edward VIII.

Donald and Margaret drove east for five days in the little Morris 8. They went from Southampton to Dover, then to Calais, Ypres, Cologne and Berlin, taking photos as they went. Inscribed on the Menin Gate, architect Edwin Lutyen's First World War memorial at Ypres, there's a Tyerman: Walter, son of William Barker and Elizabeth Tyerman (more Methodists from Osmotherley), who was killed in 1916. Less than twenty years later the land still bore clear scars of war and roads were rough and pitted. The newly completed German autobahns were off limits to civilians. Along the route, members of the Hitler Youth were greeting visitors with swastika flags for their cars. Donald and Margaret put up a pre-emptive Union Jack.

Discovering the miniature photographs with my mother's writing on the back of each one, set me off on my own visit to Berlin in 2010. I wanted to go at the same pace as my parents in 1936, so I began with a coach from Victoria station to Brussels. *Les Chemins de la Mémoire* was showing at the cinema next door to my hotel. In the morning I went by train via Cologne to Dortmund, the next day on to Hanover, and from there by coach to Berlin. My route was lined with birch, linden, larch, willow, ash and oak. As well as the trees, in these flat landscapes of north-eastern Europe there is sand, water and brick. I tried to imagine what was it like for Margaret, the only driver, making all the arrangements, ensuring access for Donald and a parking space at each overnight stop, steering for hours at a time on bone-shaking roads. Exhausting. Exciting, too.

Donald and Margaret stayed with Herr Voigt on the fourth floor of 3, Turmstrasse, near Alt-Moabit in Wedding, a working-class district in the north of the city. Margaret had organised this by writing in German to the Olympic Games visitors' committee, contacted through a German friend in Southampton. I stayed in Schlutterstrasse, in Charlottenburg, West Berlin. Andreas Schlutter was the sculptor of the white marble warriors on the gates of Schloss Charlottenburg, built for Frederick the Great. The mirror-image warriors face each other and they are naked. Their right hands are raised, brandishing swords, their left hands are tucked inside their shields. Their pose is both warrior and athlete: war and beauty. Incredibly, the Charlottenburg warrior-as-discus-thrower was still used as the poster image for the 1948 London Olympic Games, so soon after the war. In Berlin's Pergamon Museum I saw the spear-carriers, the head of the discus-thrower and the Polycleitos torso from 400BC. These ancient works were acquired by the museum in 1926, only ten years before the Olympic Games. The Grecian theory of physical perfection, proportion and movement, power and seduction, was fresh in Berliners' minds.

An Olympiastadion was built in 1913 by Oscar March for the cancelled 1916 Games. His son Werner completely rebuilt it for the 1936 Games, with limestone brought up from Bavaria. The stadium stands in a direct east-west line from the Brandenburg Gate, the fantasy of an eternal road along which the Reich would stretch forever. Margaret found a car park on the western side of the stadium, nearest to their seats in Block 21. They quickly discovered that it was reserved for the SS, the armed wing of the Nazi Party. Yet they were given permission to remain. Small courtesies were still possible.

During the Games Hitler had a balcony on the third level of the stadium, entered via a long flight of stairs. The torch relay from Greece to Germany was his innovation, a clever and powerful link between modern athletics and an ancient ideal. For the first time mobile outdoor radio units made it possible to broadcast the Games live around the world. Hitler also commissioned Leni Riefenstahl, a champion skier herself, to film the Games. *Olympia* was shot in 1936 but not shown till the summer of 1938. It took more than eighteen months to edit the million feet of film.

Part 1 begins with Greek sculpture coming to life. We see the journey of the flame and the sounding of the bell in the stadium to herald its arrival. Field events were shown as the most ideal: single bodies in motion, the beauty and control of physical movement. It was not about speed. Jumping and throwing were more beautiful than running. Athletes wear round spectacles, spectators wear silk toppers, boaters, bowlers, caps, and their clothing appears to be white. There are basins of water at the stadium for the athletes at the end of the marathon, a race accompanied on the film by Richard Strauss's *Olympic Hymn*, a choral fanfare with rousing intervals and syncopated rhythms. We see processing, singing, dancing, lights, the playing of fanfares, the flame in its dish, flags waving against the sky.

Riefenstahl used thirty cameramen and their work is striking: high and low angles, hidden points of view, long shots and close-ups, slow motion, shots from a balloon dirigible and from underwater. There is patterning, visual symmetries of movement so pure they seem abstract. The images exert a power that transcends specific contexts. They manipulate your senses. They are hard to resist. You know what's going on but you are charmed.

In Part 2 male athletes run by a lake. There is naked swimming and showering, glistening skin, water falling. Women are shown with their hair blowing beneath the wind and sky, among the cornfields. There's dancing, symmetry and anonymity – the single athlete and the controlled movement of a body – attention to shape, movement, coordination, line and strength, like flying. We close in on shoulders, arms, elbows, hairstyles. There's no rush. Even in the running events movement and shape predominate over speed. The poetic repetition of water and sky, shining brass, the lit stadium, the bell, the searchlights, the flame, the singing and dancing, the flags, laurels and bodies – all imply something eternal.

Olympia worships the ideal body of an Aryan athlete, directly descended from the perfection of ancient Greece. The racism is clear and disturbing. But unlike *The Triumph of the Will*, Riefenstahl's film of the Nuremberg Rallies, though there are many shots of flags in *Olympia*, there are few direct shots of Nazi insignia. The focus is on idealised bodies not swastikas. The power of the film is more erotic than political.

Donald and Margaret shouted and waved as the British team, including Godfrey Rampling (father of actress Charlotte), raced to their gold medals in the 4 x 400 metres relay and were then crowned with laurels. They gasped when one of the German women dropped the baton in their 4 x 100 metres event. Riefenstahl cuts to Hitler thumping his knee in anger. High up in the visitors' section of the stadium, Donald and Margaret also cheered Jesse Owens to his victory in the 100 metres, the first of his four gold medals. All around them people cried 'Ovvens, Ovvens'. Owens had a magical smile and was popular for his manner as well as his performance. The wide boulevard running up to the Olympiastadion station in Berlin was later re-named in his honour: Jesse-Owens-Allee. So different from his experience at home in the States where black and white athletes were segregated during competitions. Owens was only able to represent the US because he had moved to live in a Northern State. He received no official recognition after his unique Olympic success. Promises of employment were broken. He was still a black American.

When I arrived in the vast arena of the Olympiastadion I felt sick. I stood at the very place where my parents stood more than seventy years before and I felt the gravitational pull of Berlin's history. I parked my bike not far from where Margaret parked her car in 1936. Hitler's box has been demolished but other features remain: the arrowhead clock and the massive bell, cracked and fallen to the ground after a fire in 1948.

Two photos of Donald show him in the stadium, smiling and natty in black polo-neck jumper and white jacket, then smiling and trampish in his long brown mac, binoculars round his neck. Two of Margaret show her looking elegant in a sleek coat and dress, then awkward in white socks and a mannish shirt and tie.

Donald felt the simple thrill of being there. In a *Times* leader on the London Olympic Games of August 1948 Donald described: 'the electric dash of the hundred yards, the agony of the quarter, the strain of the half, and the strategy of the mile – all these must be seen in the flesh for real understanding of the nervous energy they call out and for the human drama.' Here is the declaration of his love for athletics.

Walking along the south side of the Tiergarten I came across the headquarters of the Nazis' 'Euthanasie Programme', known as 'Aktion T4' because of its address: Tiergartenstrasse, 4. Support for sterilising the 'worthless' grew during the 1930s.

Donald and Margaret in Berlin, August 1936

'Paralysis' was one of the criteria. Run by Dr Karl Brandt, Hitler's personal doctor, and Philipp Bouhler, head of Hitler's private Chancellery, Aktion T4 began work in the autumn of 1939. By 1941 there were more than 70,000 victims. By 1945, the unofficial estimate was more than 200,000. Yet Donald did not experience hostility in Berlin that summer, so smoothly was the public face of the Olympic Festival maintained for foreign visitors of whatever physique.

I first saw sections of the Berlin Wall alongside the canal and cemetery opposite the Hamburger Bahnhof, now an art gallery. I also began to notice the bricks marking the position of the Wall across the rest of the city. I was surprised by how thin it was, less than a hand's breadth, enabling it to bend like a thread. And there were two walls, each side of a no man's land containing mines, alarms, wire, searchlights, guards, dogs. One reason for the eventual construction of the Wall was the uprising in 1953 when East German workers fought the soldiers, who were all Russian. The 'East Side Gallery' was a stretch of the Wall, sprayed with graffiti and commercialised, kitsch and trendy. Donald and Margaret returned to Berlin for a conference in May 1959, two years before the construction of the Wall between the East and West sectors of the city. In 1936 they had anticipated war. It must have been a shock more than twenty years later to see the city still divided, quartered, as it would be for another thirty.

I visited the most dreadful memorial of all: Gleis 17. A long platform at Grunewald suburban station, edged with iron plates recording the exact details of how many Jews, male or female, on which day, were sent from here, to which destination, from October 1941 to March 1945. I walked along the rusting iron lattice covering the platform and looked down to read the inscriptions. This took several hours. Silver birch trees were sprouting in the pit of the railway track. It was hard and haunting. Like nothing else.

My parents' adventure in Berlin unsettled me. So soon after their fright in Heidelberg in 1934. Didn't they know anything before they set off for Germany again? Churchill had clearly warned of the danger of Hitler in a House of Commons debate of 13 April 1933. In the same debate, Eleanor Rathbone, Independent MP for the Combined Universities, demanded an explicit statement of the government's attitude. German Jewish and Socialist refugees were already being received in France and Switzerland.

Donald was an assiduous reader of the *Economist*. This would have included the book reviews. In the summer of 1933, six months after joining the *Economist*, Douglas Jay shared editorial duties while editor Walter Layton was on holiday:

> Into my hands at the *Economist* came a very startling volume, *The Brown Book of the Hitler Terror,* anonymous…exposing the Nazis' methods with a mass of evidence, and accusing them of having started the Reichstag fire as an excuse for suppressing the German Parliament. The whole book…only confirmed in my mind the view of the Nazi leaders, which I had derived from *The Times's* Berlin correspondents. I therefore wrote a full *Economist* leader which appeared on 2 September 1933… In the post-war years when apologists for Baldwin and Chamberlain have argued that nobody could have understood the Nazis' intentions fully before 1938 and 1939… I reply that it was all perfectly clear in 1933. (*Fortune and Change*, 1980).

Some events had been reported, for example the Paris exhibition in May 1934 which marked the first anniversary of the 1933 book burning outside the Library in Berlin's Bebelsplatz, and that autumn's Nuremberg Rally. But much was not. In an unpublished memoir, Hugh Carleton Greene wrote that 'when I left school in the spring of 1929 the shadow of Hitler was casting its premonitory chill'. By January 1934, when he was working in Germany as a foreign correspondent for the *Daily Telegraph*, he wrote that 'terror had become a part of ordinary respectable bourgeois life...little men knew and buried the horror deep in their subconscious'. Greene visited Dachau concentration camp not long after it opened in 1933 and reported: 'This was evil in broad daylight'.

Christabel Bielenberg was another young English woman who, like Margaret, was married in 1934, she to Peter, a lawyer from Hamburg. In her 1970 memoir *The Past Is Myself*, she wrote:

> Events moved very fast after January 30th, 1933. The burning of the Reichstag, the banning of the Communist Party, the last free elections, the passing of the Enabling Laws, the dissolution of the Trades Unions and of all other political parties...it took Hitler exactly six months to manoeuvre himself and his Party to power... The newspapers...had become a remorseless beat of superlatives which, for me at least, defeated their purpose... I began a serious study of the London *Times*, believing sincerely, as I had been brought up to do, that it would convey to me a balanced and objective viewpoint.

What Christabel found, however, was patronising and appeasing. She came to see Germany as a 'prison turned inside out, with the criminals in command'. William Shirer shared Christabel's disillusionment. In his *Berlin Diary* he lamented that *The Times* Berlin correspondent Norman Ebbutt 'talks of quitting. He has complained to me in private that *The Times* does not print all he sends, that it does not want to hear too much of the bad side of Nazi Germany and has apparently been captivated by the pro-Nazis in London'.

Not widely known at the time was the systematic exclusion of Jewish athletes from the German Olympic team. Gretel Bergmann was the national high-jumping champion and selected for the Games. Fifteen days before they were due to start she was excluded. She soon emigrated to the United States. Martha Jacob was the javelin champion of the Jewish Sporting Youth Organisation. She was not selected. She emigrated to South Africa.

On his own journey by car to Berlin that summer of 1936, German speaker Richard Crossman, then an Oxford academic and later Labour politician and journalist, discovered for himself that behind the flags of pride and the festival of welcome for visitors, freedom of speech and action was already being censored. In the *New Statesman* later that month he described the 'Olympic Spirit' as a 'manic elation atop a ruthless suppression of the individual'.

The warnings were ignored by those who dreaded another war, by those who felt that the 1919 Versailles Treaty had been excessively harsh towards Germany, by politicians, diplomats and newspaper proprietors sympathetic to the new regime in Germany, and by those more concerned with Empire than with Europe. The flow of news to the general public was also restricted by Chamberlain's increasing control over the Press Lobby during the 1930s, by his admiration for German efficiency and by his ambition to be the one to secure the peace. Donald read the newspapers and listened to the radio but he was not yet a journalist with access to unfiltered reports. In an *Economist* leader of 29 August 1942, entitled 'Underground Germany', Donald confirmed how little was known by the general public in the mid-thirties.

Enough was known, however, for Roosevelt's Democratic US government to call for a boycott of the Games. Chicago construction tycoon Avery Brundage, ex-athlete and influential member of the International Olympic Committee, was implacably opposed. He argued that sport and politics shouldn't mix. He was also persuaded by the Germans that the situation there was better than it actually was. He wanted to believe this. For him, the Olympic Games were more important than anything else. Eric Phipps, British Ambassador in Berlin, argued the Games should go ahead because this would make for better relations with Germany. The Foreign Office did not take the boycott seriously. Neither did the BBC.

Jewish lawyer and journalist Harold Abrahams, star of the 1924 Paris Olympic Games, was originally pro-boycott but by 1935, and despite anti-Jewish riots in Berlin that year, he wanted to attend the Games. Controller of public relations and programmes at the BBC, Cecil Barnes, had to decide whether to let Abrahams, one of their best commentators, go to Berlin. 'Might it not upset the Germans? We are gentlemen, after all.' Abrahams did not officially go for the BBC. He went as 'assistant manager' of the British team. Once in Berlin, however, he did commentate for the BBC, notably on the 1500 metres final, won by New Zealand's Jack Lovelock, who was a friend. Abrahams was overtly emotional, saying: 'Jack, come on!' And 'hooray!' when he won.

Christopher Booker's study of the 1980 Moscow Olympic Games was sent to Donald for review. Moscow was another Games run as a major public relations exercise by a totalitarian regime and Booker explicitly compared Moscow 1980 to Berlin 1936. He asked if the Games would ever be free from commercial or political corruption. His answer was that political writers say no but sports writers say yes. Frustratingly for me, in his *Economist* review, anonymous as always, Donald says nothing about what it had been like to be there in Berlin.

International Olympic Games can never be simply about the running or the jumping or the swimming or the sailing. They always carry loud messages about politics and commerce, society and fashion, competition and status, nationalism and race. It is certainly a mistake, however, for political commentators to underestimate the sheer charisma of physical skill and beauty.

The year 1936 was another turning point in Donald's life. A few years earlier Oxford's Trinity College offered him a fellowship. Despite his disability he had a reputation across the university as a brilliant young man. It was when his engagement was announced in *The Times* that Trinity wrote to him withdrawing the offer. My mother said, 'We laughed like anything'. My father wanted to get married more than he wanted to be an Oxford don.

As careers adviser for his Southampton students, job advertisements came Donald's way and were discarded if not taken up. In 1936 the *Economist* was looking for an assistant editor because Douglas Jay was moving to the *Daily Herald*. Donald initially threw the notice in the bin. Then he suddenly reached down, retrieved it and applied for the job himself. Perhaps he was energised by the chance to overcome Oxford's rejection. Perhaps he was restless after the disturbing excitement of Berlin. Perhaps he saw a chance to put his research interests to good use. Perhaps it would mean a better salary. Two days after the closing date for applications Donald sent a telegram. He was interviewed on Christmas Eve by Walter Layton, Hargreaves Parkinson, Graham Hutton and Geoffrey Crowther. They hired him on the spot.

Donald had read more back numbers of the *Economist* than anyone living. His knowledge of the history and tradition of the paper, together with his academic qualifications, were more important to the senior staff than his lack of journalistic experience. Donald even carried his unfinished MPhil thesis to the interview in a brown paper parcel. Nobody asked to look at it. They only asked him if he was in the habit of reading the *Economist*. He said yes, he was. When the interview was over Donald got up and left. Layton saw the brown paper parcel on the floor and hurried out after him. Donald was young and strong in those days but I've no idea how he managed to carry the parcel while needing both hands for his sticks.

Donald's new life as a journalist meant that Margaret had to give up her own chance of an academic career. She had excelled in her undergraduate special subject on Tudor social and economic policy, tutored by Donald. After completing her obligatory teacher-training year, she began work to expand this into a PhD. I have her primary research files from 1934–6, huge black ring-binders filled with thick university stationery, detailing unpublished material for case studies on Winchester, Southampton and Portsmouth, relevant documents transcribed in pencil from sources in Latin and English. She also gave a course of ten weekly lectures on 'The World Since The War' to Workers' Educational Association students on Wednesday evenings at the grammar school in Gillingham, at a cost of 2 shillings. The curriculum she devised was ambitious, covering the 1918 Settlement, Russia, the Depression across Europe, the Far East and the near East, Africa and America, and was supported by a reading list of thirty-five substantial texts.

At the beginning of 1937 they came to live in London, Donald for the first time. Margaret was returning, though not to the Clapham of her unhappy adolescence. They rented a flat at 83, South Hill Park, Hampstead. While Donald went to the office in Bouverie Street every day, Margaret went over to Sloane Square:

> Being married it was almost impossible to get a teaching job [in practice, though not in law, there was a 'marriage bar' – wives would take work away from men, the true bread winners]. The head of the John Lewis Partnership, Spedan Lewis, had some quite advanced ideas of management, one of which was to take on graduate trainees. I spent an extremely happy two years at Peter Jones [in its brand-new building], starting in the unpacking section of the China and Glass department... One met on equal terms people from many walks of life. Much of the work was unskilled and some of it was temporary. There were people with difficult and complicated backgrounds, the money was poor and for many years there was very little security. The social mix gave one an insight into how people lived, which I would not have missed. There was no National Health Service and the Partnership ran a very good welfare service for people ill or in personal difficulty. Members of staff were given shares in the company. There was the same sort of camaraderie that one found later in the Services. Coming from a restricted background I found it exhilarating.

A Cuckoo

Civvy Street

Donald's life in wartime London was complicated, risky and exhausting. During the night of 10 May 1941 German bombing destroyed the *Economist* office in Bouverie Street and the printers' building half a mile away. It was a Saturday. The premises were empty. However, the brown paper parcel containing the 30,000 words of Donald's postgraduate thesis was destroyed. The previous October, a bomb blast threw Donald out of a taxi going up from Fleet Street to Broadcasting House in Portland Place. He wrote a note to Miss Fisher at Europa Publications near Temple Bar to let them know he wouldn't be able to call in to see them that morning as arranged. The accident was 'slight', he said, but he was going to the doctor 'for a precautionary examination' and would be back at the *Economist* the following day. On a third occasion, walking in the blackout one evening Donald put his stick through the grating of a drain. He fell and the stick broke. He asked a passer-by if he could get a replacement somewhere near. 'Yes,' said the man, helping him up, 'there's a shop right here in Fleet Street.' This turned out to be cricketing legend Jack Hobbs's retirement enterprise. Donald came out with a new stick and a cricket ball signed by the 'Master'. The ball was as precious to him as the stick.

War was declared less than three years after Donald began his new career on the *Economist*. It took me five days to list all the articles he wrote between the summer of 1941 and the autumn of 1944. Of his print journalism between 1937 and the bombing of 1941 there remains no trace. Four transformative years literally up in smoke. What followed for Donald, however, was heroic. He wrote all three leaders in eleven issues of the paper and all seven Notes in the issue of 28 February 1942, his main subjects being the economics of war and planning for post-war reconstruction in housing, education and health. Donald saw a welfare state as the fruit of dedicated pioneers who wanted the many to have the chances till now reserved for the few. The *Economist* staff would sit together round a small table in their new office high up in Brettenham House, a deco monolith in Lancaster Place, or in the coffee house on the ground floor, more comfortable than the attic. Tamara, wife of historian Isaac Deutscher, who wrote for the *Economist* in the 1940s, described these sessions as 'five men playing ping pong'.

There were multiple deadlines to keep up with rapidly changing events, Donald's health was often poor and there were frequent calls for help from his mother several hundred miles away in the North East. Communications were shaky. One colleague complained that it took five hours to get through to Donald on the telephone. There were, too, the almost daily demands of BBC radio talks, given late in the evening after a full day in the office, before dashing to catch the last train from Waterloo to his digs in the Ardmay Hotel, Adelaide Road, Surbiton.

Towards the end of 1939 Donald had launched a parallel career at the BBC. He wrote a five-page letter to Christopher Salmon, Director of Talks, pitching a series of weekly talks explaining the economics of the war simply and objectively. The BBC could do this better than the press or government leaflets, he said, and the talks would be as important for listeners in Europe and the States as for the 'Home' audience. 'This is probably presumptuous,' he wrote, 'but it is a sincere effort to help. There is a real job to be done here. This is an economic war. Millions know this. But they don't grasp much more than the general statement.' His letter ends with apologies for 'such unconscionable length'. 'You write most disarming letters,' Salmon replied. 'How did you know – but I suppose it's obvious – how much taste we have here for people of modesty'.

I am struck by the forwardness and backwardness of my father's approach. He's confident that there's an important job to be done and that he can do it. He takes the initiative. He also feints and apologises but he's 'sincere'. It worked. Between 1940 and 1941 Donald wrote and presented three talks a fortnight for the BBC. For a fee of a few guineas he went through detailed rounds of drafting, revising, rehearsing, recording or presenting live, and responding to feedback. As well as talks for the Home Service and for the Overseas Service for audiences in India, Africa and South America, Donald wrote dialogues on topical issues like rationing with 'Alf', a young lorry driver, for Schools Broadcasting. He had to be inventive to keep the system going. When he went on holiday to the Isle of Wight for

Easter 1941, he sent a talk off by itself on a train to London from Brockenhurst in Hampshire.

One twenty-minute programme generated a large and abusive post-bag. On the evening of 11 March 1940, he interviewed the economist John Maynard Keynes live on the BBC Home Service. He was just thirty-two, Keynes fifty-seven. It was the second of five programmes on 'The Economic War – what it means to us', for which Donald was general editor. An exhibition to accompany the series was set up by the Ministry of Information in the Booking Hall at Charing Cross Station. This was the eve of the retreat from Dunkirk, the fall of France and the long months of the Blitz. People were beginning to realise that the war effort needed to involve the whole economy.

Keynes outlined his scheme for compulsory savings in a talk to the Fabian Society in February. Canvassing opinion in his local pub, the BBC's Northern Regional Director (NRD), Patrick Thornhill, discovered how far Keynes had failed to sell his scheme to the trade unions and working people. The Buxton landlord asserted that there would be 'bloody revolution' if the scheme went ahead. Thornhill circulated an internal memo saying that it was 'high time we put the pros and cons…and independent of the Treasury', where the Chancellor, Sir John Simon, was also critical of Keynes. Someone popular and trusted by the TUC, Thornhill urged, so that Keynes would have to explain in words of one syllable how his proposals would affect working-class welfare. On 29 February, a memo went back to NRD. 'Not quite what you had in mind but we are asking Tyerman to represent the points likely to be of direct interest to the working man.'

There followed the collaborative toing and froing between

Donald and the BBC that I learned was typical for the preparation of a script. In his correspondence Donald was tough, self-effacing and humorous. In a long letter to BBC producer Norman Luker he apologised for all the work but added:

> I never wanted anything to go as well as I do this series. And I don't want the champagne of Keynes's visit to wash away entirely the light beer of my own discourses. It's a grand idea – and privilege – to have him, but there are at least three more to come, and we must have the whole thing in simple ABC.

Audience feedback was hostile. 'What an interesting post you're getting,' Luker wrote to Donald. 'Keep an eye out for a promising one with an accessible address. We could get the writer in. We must say something about the distress. Let's discuss soon.' A few days later Donald replied from the *Economist* office. 'Here's my talk for Monday,' he wrote, 'in MSS, no copies, because shorthanded here with the calling-up etc… I have concentrated on the letters, because they are important and because of my own desire to face up to this bitterness.' This follow-up talk was reproduced in *The Listener* on 20 March, under the title 'Produce More, Save More, Consume Less', with an introduction referring to the angry letters.

Donald received colourfully inconsistent feedback. On 8 April 1940, Thornhill sent a memo to the 'Secretary of the Central Committee for Group Listening' with a copy to Norman Luker:

> I think Tyerman is on the whole good, though he talks in a slightly gloomy tone of voice. The talk in which J. M. Keynes

appeared was, of course, the star-turn, and I only wish it could have gone on for at least half an hour.

Donald's gloomy voice is at odds with the playful confidence of his letter writing to BBC colleagues. I feel the tension of a live broadcast with an eminent person and the safety of a much-edited script, careful and precise. You wouldn't expect provocation or entertainment. Donald was the youngster but also the elucidator/ teacher, mediating the great man's ideas for a wide audience of hard-pressed ordinary people. No audible ego. And it was a serious business, the question of social justice in wartime and how to avoid the problems experienced during the First World War. The language is of fairness and government responsibilities, almost sacred tasks. When Donald said, on air or in his correspondence, that something was 'grand', I hear the loyalty to the North that he would occasionally affect for his children years later but which was then I suppose still partly automatic despite his years in Oxford and Southampton. But on the tape from 1940 I hear the voice of a young man I never knew.

The *New Zealand Observer* was appalled: 'Of all the BBC commentators none can give me the willies so completely as Mr. Donald Tyerman. His voice has the quality of lard… His manner is that of an elderly scout master [Donald was thirty-four] giving the lads a chat on morale.'

There's a grittier tone in Donald's correspondence with the BBC for a talk on British-German trade for the Overseas Service in August 1940 ahead of a speech to be given in the House of Commons by Trade Minister Anthony Greenwood. Donald was asked for 800 words. A week later he received a note from Miss Barker, not a BBC staff member but a civil servant in the Ministry of Information, in response to his draft: 'It was perhaps more simple and rather less factual than we really wanted but I expect that was mainly due to a lack of suitable facts. Anyhow I think you will achieve a valuable purpose and I have only made very slight changes and cuts.' Donald sent a handwritten postcard in reply: 'I'm sorry it was too simple. I'm afraid I hadn't realised that, in order to address the Serbo-Croats, it was advisable to be more complex than I am when speaking every week to the great British public.'

Wartime broadcasting played to Donald's strengths: simplicity, warmth, collaboration, concentration, reading aloud, at ease sitting in the studio. In theory, broadcasting was also flexible – talks could be prepared quickly in response to changing circumstances. In practice, however, as Donald pointed out with irritation, the printing schedules of the *Radio Times* often wiped out this advantage.

Donald called his radio talks 'my pigeons', flying off to deliver information and analysis and bringing home valuable feedback. There were many attractions. The audience was huge, about 1,400,000 listeners compared to the estimated 180,000 readers of a popular Penguin book, or the much smaller, though select, readership of the *Economist*. And on the radio he spoke in his own voice and name.

It is easy to forget the reach of the BBC and the influence of weekly journals in those days. Donald was at the centre of both in his early thirties, during the crucial wartime years. He had his international by-line on air and his anonymous authority in print. This would have been extraordinary for someone who began with all life's advantages. For someone who nearly fell down a Fleet Street pothole in the blackout, it was truly heroic.

*

The year 1943 was exceptional. I saw him propelling himself between endlessly demanding parallel activities and I tried to imagine how he felt when the death of a brother detonated a personal hole in the midst of it all. He edited both the *Economist* and the *Observer*, he broadcast for the BBC and he edited and contributed to three books: *Ways and Means of Rebuilding*, the Report of the Town and Country Planning Association's July conference, *Industry After The War* by Mass Observation co-founder Charles Madge, and the volume of essays marking the *Economist*'s Centenary, 1843–1943.

From Monday to Thursday Donald edited the *Economist*. In that one year he wrote 52 *Economist* leaders and 182 Notes. He wrote all three leaders for the issues of 3 April, 25 September, 9 October and 16 October. He was by now living with Margaret in Essex and he commuted daily into Liverpool Street station. An office car would take him along Threadneedle Street to Queen Victoria Street, then down Ludgate Hill, up Fleet Street and around the Aldwych to Lancaster Place at the top of The Strand. Every day Donald rode through the devastated streets of the City, the wrecked landscape for all his professional endeavours.

In 'Leaving a Void Behind' (7 August 1943) Donald warned that, though he won the war, Churchill might lose the peace. He objected to statements made by Churchill in his radio broadcast on 'Britain after the First World War'. Donald warned of the consequences of not being ready for post-war reconstruction. In a cutting tone, Donald argued that the war was prepared by 'committees of coordinators' and now the peace was being prepared by 'study groups'. Just as air mastery was at the heart of the Allies war plan, economics should be at the centre of the 'campaign for reconstruction'. We need Bills now, he argued, not 'wireless orations'. It was Churchill's choice and character to govern with a minimum of delegation and he has been vindicated:

> …but the bottleneck is still there on his desk, shifted from the planning of war, which he has accomplished, to the planning of peace, which he has set aside. The time has come now when for peace, too, he must decide or delegate. The Prime Minister is one of a brief band of great British leaders who have led their country to success against great odds. It would be a melancholy epilogue for Mr. Churchill to go down as the Prime Minister who won the greatest war in British history, and then lost the peace.

On Fridays and Saturdays Donald edited the *Observer*. The office was in Tudor Street, round the corner from Bouverie Street and the Blitzed *Economist*. David Astor, second son of the paper's owner, Waldorf, and destined to work on the *Observer*, was twenty-nine and in the Armed Forces, first as a Marine, and then in the Special Operations Executive (SOE).

After the departure of the paper's long-serving editor, J.L.Garvin, in February 1942, several people filled the gap. The following year, however, David told his father that senior members of staff were complaining about the *Observer*'s erratic editorial policy and the lack of follow-up on main stories. There were no editorial meetings and a frequent change of editor. David suggested bringing in Donald, who had been recommended to him by Donald's *Economist* colleague, Barbara Ward. Donald was appointed in August.

Editorial independence and writing of exceptional quality characterised the *Observer* during Donald's time as editor. The paper took a particularly independent line on foreign affairs, including sustained opposition to de Gaulle, whom it saw as proto-Fascist, and to the Soviet expansion in Eastern Europe, which the government refused to take seriously. On 9 January 1944 the *Observer* was the only paper to publicise the Soviet takeover of Poland, breaking a Ministry of Information embargo.

Soon after Donald began working on the *Observer* David Astor was describing him as 'the most valuable man we have. He is definitely worthy of the editorship'. However, 'the only catch is that that cancels out my post-war vocation.' He wanted to edit the paper himself but 'the prospect of Tyerman leaving the paper before I am free to take over fills me with dismay and apprehension'. Astor's ambivalence grew during the spring of 1944. He told Tom Jones, long-serving Deputy Secretary to the Cabinet and Waldorf Astor's great friend and advisor, that he wanted to be the 'full-blown editor', with Donald as political editor and Ivor Brown as cultural editor. David Astor claimed that Donald had admitted excluding him from discussions, adding that Donald 'has treated me so sharply and with such prickly suspicion from the start'. Jones replied, saying that much of Donald and Ivor Brown's resentment was caused by 'the unmeasured criticism you hurled at them' and that Donald was rightly apprehensive, given David's power over appointments. Jones hoped that Brown would be able to persuade Donald to stay on the paper and accept 'you on top', adding that 'Tyerman has brought strength and precision to the leading articles'.

Donald left the *Observer* in September 1944 but he maintained a friendship with the Astor family. They congratulated him on his appointment as editor of the *Economist* in 1955. Now Donald could broadcast again. David Astor wrote from his home in St John's Wood to Ian Jacob, Director General of the BBC, assuring him that Donald was equally good on radio or television and in talks or discussions:

> I know him well. He has a clear and straightforward mind and a simple, incisive and very sensible way of expressing himself. I think his personality is striking without being showy. His judgment always seemed to me to be excellent. If the BBC made use of Tyerman it would be some compensation for having turned Malcolm Muggeridge into a national figure.

In 1979 Donald received the Astor Award for his work in the Commonwealth Press Union and when he died in 1981, the Astor family wrote warmly to my mother. In the late 1990s, a few years before he himself died, David Astor saw my youngest brother at a party in Oxford. He made a point of going over to him and speaking affectionately about our father.

I have my mother's copy of the Oxford University Press navy-blue hardback published in 1943 to celebrate the *Economist*'s Centenary, inscribed: 'Margaret / D. September 2nd, 1943, from the Deputy Editor', the initials, as always, scrupulously underlined as if for the printers. The frontispiece is a portrait of James Wilson, founder of the paper in 1843 and its first editor, who ran the paper from 340, The Strand, round the corner from post-Blitz Brettenham House and close to the refurbished Adelphi building into which the *Economist* moved in 2017. The 1843 masthead announced a 'Political, Literary and General Newspaper' and contents included economics, parliamentary debates, weekly news, cultural notices, law reports, book reviews and letters. Donald describes this as the 'embryo' of a journal of public affairs written by political economists. In the 1840s the *Economist* carried advertisements for needles, fishhooks, inks, maps, microscopes, books, pianos, mineral waters, cutlery, baths, tablecloths, tailors, Parr's Life Pills, Rowland's Macassar Oil and Hall's Galoshes.

Donald's chapter, 'A Hundred Years', was co-written with A.H. Chapman, repository of *Economist* folklore since 1898. The anonymity of the paper was important, Donald argued, guaranteeing more continuity, balanced judgment and influence than the modern fashion for 'a parade of names'. But producing the *Economist* was not a 'mystic and impersonal process,' he said. People mattered too. The worth of the paper derived from the qualities of the actual men and women.

Wilson, editor from 1843 to 1859, and Walter Bagehot, editor from 1859 to 1877, were both bankers. Bagehot married one of Wilson's six daughters. Neither man was primarily a journalist. Wilson was an MP, Bagehot was a 'giant of Victorian letters'. The longest-serving editor (Edward Johnstone, 1883–1907) was a financial specialist. After Wilson's death in 1860 the paper was owned by the Trust he set up for his daughters. Donald's thumbnail sketch brings them alive: 'there is no more picturesque feature in the history of any modern newspaper than the gentle proprietorship of these long-lived ladies.'

The Centenary issue of the paper itself was entitled 'Towards the Second Century'. Donald's leader, 'Active Citizenship', compares relative freedoms in Britain and Russia at the time of the 1941 Anglo-Soviet alliance. In Russia, he wrote, you couldn't criticise or oppose government, but workers could dismiss their bosses. In Britain, people didn't feel they were active participants, though it should be 'the common principle'. Some people envy Soviet workers' councils, though these were 'more than a little idealised'. 'The organisation of total war has made it plainer than ever before that the few make policy and govern while the many do what they are told'. Donald argued that there were 'new ways to involve ordinary people', especially young people. In peacetime the challenge was to keep alive the public spirit and sense of civic duty awakened by war through 'genuine and universal' equal opportunities in education, work and public service.

Franklin Delano Roosevelt, American President and regular reader of the *Economist*, sent a telegram: 'Hearty congratulations to you and your associates on the Centenary of *The Economist*... In the great task of economic enlightenment *The Economist* can play a significant part.'

My initial view of this prolific year was mistaken. Donald's journalism and broadcasting, together with all the additional writing, editing and consulting, didn't so much represent a year of rushing between disparate jobs as it did the unstinting pursuit of a set of overarching priorities: making life better for ordinary men, women and children, rebuilding for the future rather than recreating the past, repeatedly pressing the government for vital decisions on post-war reconstruction, fighting on all fronts for a close-knit fabric of social democracy. This was Donald's active service.

As it was for the war, 1943 was a pivotal year for Donald personally, encompassing some of the best and the worst experiences of his life. In 1944, he was lured away from both weeklies, the *Economist* and the *Observer*. In any case, demobilisation would enable David Astor to take up his inheritance at the *Observer*, as Foreign Editor in 1945 and as editor from 1948, while Geoffrey Crowther had already returned to his Editor's chair at the *Economist*. As he became a father for the first time, Donald became Assistant Editor on *The Times*. He moved to take up 'the biggest job on earth'.

Letters from Africa

Harry was the youngest of the three Tyerman brothers, born in 1912. By the outbreak of war in 1939 he was married to Connie, living in County Durham and working for Pearl Assurance while she worked for a bank. Harry was reluctant to join up but Donald's journalism changed his mind. In one *Economist* leader, Donald discussed the new National Service Bill. He argued that 'the distinction between the armed forces and other national service, which is in any case somewhat unreal in a total war economy, is by now blurred…the obligation now rests upon every citizen to serve'. By March 1940 Harry had enlisted in the Yorkshire Light Infantry. Twenty-three years after the sailor suit and drooping socks, he was handsome in a soldier's uniform. Harry wrote letters home to Connie, his mother Catherine, and his brothers Reg and Don. A dozen survive. Eight of the twelve, dated July 1940 to April 1943, were written to Catherine. His letters to Connie are lost.

By March 1943 Harry was in North Africa, where the Germans had recently defeated the Allies at Sidi Bou Zid and the Kasserine Pass. Catherine was now living with Donald and Margaret in Essex. He sent love to her but no news. Only that he'd been in a ship 'for ages', that the food was good and he was very fit. 'One day I'll tell you about it all.' He assumed Donald would be reading the letter, too, so he added: 'All the best to you, Don. I'll run across your voice in some odd corner.'

The soldiers did not know much about what was happening and censorship stopped Harry from writing about the little he did know. His addresses were coded sets of numbers and initials. He wrote about the weather. He saw Arabs 'dressed in rags and living in unbelievable hovels'. At first he was amazed to hear them speaking French but his letters reveal a growing understanding. The country is 'much more green than I anticipated,' he wrote to his older brother Reg 'the people much poorer than I anticipated. One reason for their rags is that, since the Vichy Commission, the country has been cleaned out of all reserves. Money isn't much use here. Eggs and oranges are bought with cigarettes.' Harry was looking forward to the 'great day' when he and Connie could set up house on their own again.

By the beginning of April, Harry told his mother that he was 'rotting away with boredom'. He'll go mad. There was bathing in the local hot springs. He visited a small town – 'dirty, shops empty, restaurants closed, Arabs and French doing nothing'. He found a new watch glass and parts for a broken lamp and his French was well up to the negotiations. He talked to an Arab mechanic, who told him he worked from 8am to 8pm for 5 francs a day, for himself, his wife, two children and his parents, and that he had hens and figs of his own. Harry said: 'the Arab looked quite French.' He still hadn't received any letters from England.

On 11 April 1943, Harry told Donald he'd heard Geoffrey Crowther on the 9 o'clock News. 'It seems that economists are being forced to accept – or rather they hope to force nations to accept the fact that the only ultimate cure of economic ills is for the more fortunate ones to give to the poorer ones. No doubt the two plans suggested by America and England will have caused a stir in your paper'. Harry listened to the news regularly. 'Thank the Lord it is good news.'

On 13 April Harry received the first letter from home, from his mother, dated 4 March. The next day he wrote to his nephew Roy aged nine, ill with scarlet fever. 'This is a funny land. Little arab boys speak French'. He told Roy about the warm springs and the orange trees. In one of his earlier letters to Reg he had included a message for Roy telling him about all the different soldiers he'd seen: American, French, English, Scots, even 'some black troops'. He signed himself 'Uncle Harry', which he would never be to us, Donald's post-war children. The elder of my two brothers is Robert Harry.

There was camaraderie in the desert but Harry was homesick. Letters from his family were not getting through. 'Back for Christmas?' he asked. 'Unlikely. Never mind, it will be a festive day when we do arrive.' He was married and, at thirty-one, older than most of the men and perhaps even now did not really share their commitment. He had never been abroad before. He dreamed of coming home. 'I have already found that the bright light of the future, shining through all my conscious hours, is the journey back.'

Lieutenant Tyerman was killed by a sniper on 24 April. Connie received the carbon copy of a handwritten telegram from the Under Secretary of State for War on the evening of 4 May. She wrote at once to her brother-in-law Reg asking him to tell the family. She says: 'I may go away somewhere for a few days – <u>please</u> don't let anyone try to see me. You will feel this so much and my heart goes out to you both.' My mother believed that 'to the end of her life she blamed Don for Harry's death'. Yet only a few years later she agreed to be my second godmother. I think my father wrote to Connie hoping she would feel able to rejoin the family, even in this small way, and accept his overture as an acknowledgement of their shared grief.

Harry's grave is in Massicault War Cemetery, about twenty miles outside Tunis, a sloping green field of perfectly tended white graves commemorating hundreds of young men from a quite different country, powerful memories cut adrift. My nephew James visited Harry's grave in 2012, guided there by a sketch Uncle Reg made on a British Legion visit in the 1970s.

'Out of Africa', Donald's front-page *Economist* leader for 15 May 1943, began with the words: 'Africa is free'. Less than a month after Harry's death, these three words were true. Eisenhower had defeated the Germans at Thala, heralding victory in North Africa at last.

Donald had written about Tunisia before. On 31 October 1942, he observed that progress had been made against Rommel but the outcome remained uncertain. On 9 January 1943, he was still downbeat. There were 'shortages, inertia, lack of military coordination', 'tactical light-mindedness', 'premature action'. Donald noted the inexperience of the Allied troops compared to the veteran Axis men and he urged General Eisenhower to act quickly. On 1 May, Donald wrote that 'Progress in Tunisia since the capture of Enfidaville has been painfully slow, but sure'. There were reports of a renewed Eighth Army offensive but overall it was stalemate. In a Note on the question of early demobilisation in the same issue, Donald estimated that the war's end was 'still a very long time distant'.

Yet by mid-May he could write that 'the last Axis army in Africa collapsed almost overnight'. 'This is the real turning of the tide, the transformation signalled by the triumph of Alamein and the Allied landings six months ago, and made possible by the prodigious resistance of the Russians'. It demonstrated the 'strength of industrial democracy against totalitarian aggression... These have been perilous times in the desert. The achievement is vast.' After praising the Allies' leadership and their machinery of warfare, Donald argued that 'it was a soldier's victory'.

'Out of Africa' reads to me like the funeral oration to Harry he was never able to give. Donald writes as if he is speaking or even

Lieutenant Tyerman in uniform, 1942 (L)
His grave in Tunisia, 1943 (R)

chanting. In places the text resembles a hymn to 'the men who die in freedom's armies':

> Tunisia is a symbol of hope, as well as of strength and unity. Behind the clangour of the victory bells there is the mournful rolling of the muffled drum and it will swell as the advance goes on. The debt of Dunkirk has been paid, as the King has said. The young men who died or were crippled on those harsh Tunisian hillsides ask for no fine words or memorials, no vicarious play with their sufferings and sacrifice, no wordy pledges. With their comrades of Norway, Belgium, France, Greece, Crete, Malaya and Burma, with the few of the Battle of Britain, with the many of Russia's resistance, with the sufferers of subjugated Europe and the stricken far east, with all those lost by sea, on land and in the air, they want what they went out to fight for – a sure end to the war. They have expiated the sloth and blindness of other men. They have given their lives and their vigour that others, more fortunate, may finish the job. The men who die or are crippled in freedom's armies are ordinary men with ordinary homes and families and ordinary aspiration. They hate war, they fight to get it over. Something new must surely come this time out of Africa, something new and strong and resolute and full of hope that will enable the world at last to ensure the peace it seeks.

Thirty-eight years later, in 1981, Donald, the brother who would become my father, died on 24 April.

Soldier-Mother

Margaret was the one in uniform.

> War seemed inevitable so plans had to be made. Don, having
> polio, could not join up. We decided, having no children, it was
> right that I should volunteer. Like most of our friends we had
> been passionately against war and supported the aims of the
> Peace Pledge Union. There was great heart-searching but as the
> horrors of the Nazi regime became known in England many
> felt that it was too great an evil to be ignored.

She volunteered for the Auxiliary Territorial Services (ATS),
one of the first women to do so when it was formed in 1938 after
Chamberlain returned from Munich. She was called up on 2
September 1939, the day before war was declared. She was twenty-six.

Margaret in uniform, 1940

In the official photographs she still has the shy smile of her schooldays, with a clear, unmarked face, open, direct, awkward. Looking at them is unsettling. It could be me rather than Margaret. More like a me I remember than a mother I remember, for I didn't know this young woman at all though she's so familiar. 'Being in the army was in many ways like a return to childhood,' she wrote later, 'like being at school…rules and regulations, ranks, promotions, fuss over uniform.' As a junior officer Margaret found it hard 'to enforce rules for which I could not find a reason'. She remembered being sent on a course 'at the end of which a group photograph was taken for the War Office files. I got an official letter from the War Office complaining that my cap was at an angle.'

They put the furniture from their South Hill Park flat into storage. Margaret handed her crockery over to a neighbour who said it would get broken otherwise, so she'd take care of it. When Margaret sent a van round to collect it after the war the woman gave the driver a poker, saying that was all Margaret had left.

Before they left London, Margaret and Don had a farewell drink at the Freemasons Arms in Downshire Hill. In the 1970s, my husband Alex and I would often walk over from Tufnell Park to the Freemasons Arms to meet my parents for a drink before Sunday lunch at the flat in West End Lane. The pub was spacious and accessible. Parking was easy. My parents never once mentioned that they had lived round the corner or told us any of their wartime stories. The *Reminiscences* Ma wrote in the 1980s were a revelation. These few pages contain such a vivid account of her life as a young woman, her only personal record.

At first Margaret was billeted in an empty house in Hornton Street, Kensington, which soon became known as The Bug House.

'We came out in spots. The C.O. thought we had caught measles and called the M.C. He took one look at us and laughed. We were deloused. I wonder what the present owners [1980s] would think about that.' It was the details of 'how we lived in that strange time' that stuck in her mind. 'Broken glass, wrecked houses were commonplace. One silly memory – after a nearby raid some of the houses in Kensington High Street were hit, including a furrier's. Fox furs were strewn in a line across the street, like a pack of wild animals.' Another memory: 'There was an old lady living nearby who was very kind to us, providing hot baths, meals at odd times and generally befriending us. One night during the raids a bomb fell and the only direct hit was on her house. The abnormal became the normal.'

Margaret was a driver. 'I was given an old laundry van, with one useable gear.' When the evacuation from Dunkirk started, Margaret and her van were sent to Addison Road Station, later Olympia. She remembered 'a great feeling of relief and excitement that so many, apart from exhaustion, were in good shape. One man from the Guards said to me 'I'm sorry we've let you down'. She also remembered 'a very pretty and elegant blonde sent by Horlicks, who offered everyone in sight a hot drink. I tend to associate Horlicks with Dunkirk'. Margaret saw military police taking a man off one of the trains. 'We were told he was suspected of being a spy. He was wet, dirty and dishevelled but they said his feet were dry. He had not been in the water.' The drivers cheered each train as it came in and when the message came that there would be no more trains, 'we refused to believe it and had to be ordered out. We waited just in case another train came…it did not.'

Margaret wasn't above moonlighting: delivering Jaffa Juice

round the suburbs of North London. When historian Isaac Deutscher was first in England he wrote articles in Polish that were translated by his friend Eric Sosnow, whose English was slightly better. Together they would go and see Donald at the *Economist*, where he paid them 10 shillings an article. Margaret remembered:

> Eric was the kind of person who in a war does well because he would turn his hand to anything... Before the war was over and Israel was just starting up, he got the concession to import Jaffa Juice into England, and he took a little factory, one shed on the North Circular Road, and he and a woman bottled this orange juice. I used to take an army truck round and get great vats of it. And that's how Eric started, he was quite a romantic figure in the business world.

When they had to go down into the cellars during the Blitz, the ATS junior officers discussed what to wear. Their uniforms were made by Huntsman's of Savile Row. 'Some argued that we should take the best one, then, if the building was blown up and we were dug out, we would have on our best clothes.'

Later, Margaret spent six months in at the Dreghorn Barracks in Edinburgh, training young conscripts to drive: 'Trying to teach girls to drive ambulances on narrow steep roads was a test of nerve. Many of the recruits had never ridden in a car and had absolutely no road sense'. October to May on the Pentland Hills was freezing, too. They went to bed in their greatcoats and off-duty hours were spent gathering wood for the stove. They were vaccinated against smallpox which had broken out in the city. What Margaret remembered most about Edinburgh in those days, however, was how unfriendly people were to her cockney recruits. 'Coming from the South, as most of us did, we were not popular and I do not remember ever being invited into a private house. The glamorous Free Poles, some of whom were high-class Counts, were greatly in demand. But there was a small place, Penycuik, where the local ladies always gave us hot drinks as we chugged through in badly driven convoys.'

I wonder if she saw Leslie Howard's 1943 film *The Gentle Sex*. I came across it when I read the obituary of Joyce Howard, one of the stars. I booked myself into the British Film Institute Archive's basement off Tottenham Court Road for a viewing. The film shows the ATS as a melting pot of women from different social classes and argues that their contribution to the war should be taken seriously. Over a scene of three women operating an anti-aircraft battery, Howard's voice says: 'Before Waterloo women only appeared at the Ball. Now, without women we couldn't carry on.'

Women were vital to overall manpower policy during the years of acute crisis. Between June 1941 and October 1942, Donald wrote twelve articles in the *Economist* on women in the Army. Assumptions by journalists and politicians that these women were naturally represented by female MPs or that being in uniform was 'unwomanly' he dismissed as 'silly season gossiping' and 'muddle-headed muttering'. The ATS was integral to the Army, he argued, and their gender was irrelevant to doing a proper job as trained professionals; they were entitled to high self-esteem. Moreover, for each woman aged between twenty and thirty without children who enlisted or undertook essential war work, a man was released for armed service.

For some years after the war Margaret sustained the friendships she made in the ATS. Some were known to us, as they were to each other, by their surnames: Miles, Eccles. Her closest wartime friends, though, were Teff, who didn't marry the man she was supposed to, and Joey, Irish and dynamic, with her tiny red sports car. She became my godmother, as Eccles was godmother to my sister Mary. We visited Miles's threadbare market garden and we visited Eccles's ramshackle house where she bred Border terriers and seemed to share their food. They were resourceful women, whose frugality was a sign of their personalities as well as their post-war struggles.

After Golders Green, Margaret was posted to Anti-Aircraft Command Headquarters at Hylands House, near Chelmsford in Essex. She was billeted in the Chase Hotel, Ingatestone, and cycled out to her base at Writtle every day. Donald was lodging in Surbiton and commuting to Fleet Street from the station at the end of the road. He would travel out to Ingatestone for the weekend when he could. Margaret found it a 'very friendly place…everyone had been uprooted, most were in the Air Force and their families joined them. Don could still manage to travel up to London so we decided to buy a house there and settle down to family life.'

Their new life in Essex at first included Donald's mother Catherine. Her health had been poor for some time. Donald had been up to Middlesbrough several times to see her in the summer of 1940, visits that had been exhausting, disruptive and dangerous. As Donald wrote to his BBC producer to explain the delay in a radio script on 'Oil': 'My mother in the North is very ill and I have been twice to see her. Now I'm called away again tonight to see her.' Ten days earlier he had told them that 'owing to a combination of wartime night travelling, air raid alarms and family anxiety, I had no sleep at all on Friday, Saturday or Sunday nights.' They invited Catherine down to stay with them in Essex. Donald and Margaret were both working full time. Catherine did not adjust well to living in the village: she felt either abandoned or used.

Margaret suffered a miscarriage in 1943. A year later, she was again pregnant. Now Catherine began to set traps for Margaret, hoping she would fall down the stairs and lose this second baby. Catherine was dispatched back up to Middlesbrough where she lived for the last eight years of her life.

Life in Ingatestone was simple. I have their ration books for 1943–6. But for Margaret it was rewarding, too. They lived in Brandiston, a Georgian house right on the village high street, part of the old Roman road from London to Colchester. They made friends with neighbours, Dorothy and Bernard Lawrence, half a generation older, and their three young children. When Margaret spoke at the Lawrence's joint memorial service in the village church of St Edmund and St Mary in 1988, she said: 'They were very good to us on many levels, giving advice, lending sugar and mending fuses'. Not only neighbours, the Lawrences were also mentors, almost substitute parents. They had come to Ingatestone in 1936, when Bernard was appointed Chief Education Officer for Essex. Margaret remembered him playing 'endless games of cricket' with his children, telling them stories and, with Donald, 'discussing with optimism the new world we hoped for or arguing over the Test Match.'

In this spirit Margaret and Donald joined the League of Nations Association, following Bernard's example. Their local branch of what became the United Nations Association was very popular, 'as we were able to coerce our friends to give talks in return for a weekend in the country. We all hoped that with patience, common sense and goodwill, we really could help to make a better world, dependent on kindness and a hope that nations could live together without hate, that life had a lot to offer if people were better educated and, therefore, have more understanding of other people's problems.'

The Lawrences encouraged Margaret's public life. She became a school governor and a governor of the Technical College in Chelmsford. And, at the age of thirty-three she was elected as an Independent Progressive to Chelmsford Rural District Council, one of the first two women ever to be elected there. She had declined the chance to become a parliamentary candidate for the Chelmsford constituency. Local Conservatives tried to discredit her by announcing that she was married to a 'Communist'. In fact, Donald and Margaret were friends of Sir Hubert Ashton, who became Tory MP for Chelmsford in 1950 and of Norman St John-Stevas, who succeeded him in 1964.

Margaret's experiences as an army officer and as a young mother were the core of her election manifesto in April 1946 (capitals as in the leaflet):

HAVING SERVED BOTH IN THE RANKS AND AS AN OFFICER, I UNDERSTAND THE MANY COMPLEX PROBLEMS OF SERVICE MEN AND WOMEN RE-TURNING TO CIVILIAN LIFE.

As a married woman, looking after a husband and a small child, as well as taking part in village activities, I know the local interests and difficulties of housewives and families.

I AM SPECIALLY CONCERNED ABOUT PRESENT HOUSING CONDITIONS, SANITATION AND WATER SUPPLY.

Margaret tells us that it's a long time since there was a contest for the election of councillors and argues that everyone on the Parliamentary Register has a duty to vote. 'I ask for that vote in support of a SOUND PROGRESSIVE POLICY.'

In the late forties, Margaret and Donald moved away from their house on the main road, up to Fryerning Lane and an inter-war brick villa called More House. One of Bernard Lawrence's passions was the collection and use by schoolchildren of local records, which led to annual exhibitions of maps and documents in Ingatestone Hall, owned, as was the village itself, by the Roman Catholic Petre family. Donald's fascination for Thomas More grew as a result of these connections. Copies of the Holbein drawings of More and his father hung in his study. More's *Dialogue of Comfort Against Tribulation* was read by my brother Christopher at his funeral.

These years in Essex were the beginning of my life, too. I rode on my father's three-wheeler when I was as young as he was when he had polio. This was a bath-chair, upholstered in black leather, which he propelled by moving two levers in contrary motion, forwards and backwards, one in each hand as he sat. There was a long floating platform for his feet, supported at the far end by a small front wheel that acted as a rudder. Dad controlled this by twisting the horizontal handle on the right-hand lever. Behind the seat of the chair was a large boot with a lid. He always carried a plastic mac, a couple of books and a radio. I sat on the platform as he sang to ease the considerable effort of moving up the lane. 'Speed bonny boat like a bird on the wing, onward the sailors cry, carry the lad who's born to be king, over the sea to Skye.'

Images of my early childhood in Essex come from the letters my father wrote to my then teenage cousin, Roy, uncle Reg's son. Uncle

Three sisters, Ingatestone, 1948

Don told Roy about our new house. He described the fields and the trees, the ducks and the moorhens on the pond, and the dog 'Pickles'. He invited Roy to come and stay during his Easter holidays. He sent the train times from Newcastle to King's Cross, then from Liverpool Street to Ingatestone and enclosed the fare. In a letter congratulating Roy on his School Certificate, Donald told him that Anne was about to start at the village school.

Anne had a teddy bear whose name was Shuttleworth. She remembered the name but had no idea where it came from. Cousin Roy knew. When my mother drove down to Ingatestone station to collect my father from the late train, Anne would sometimes go along for the ride, taking her teddy. The stationmaster would come out of his house to see if my father needed any help to get down. His name was Mr Shuttleworth. Uncle Don described in one letter how he would get home from work as late as 1 or 2 in the morning only to be woken by us children three hours or so later. He told Roy that I was becoming 'more and more of a rascal everyday'. The following summer, however, Donald upgraded this and, yet again, observed that Anne and I had inherited his 'wild rages'.

Donald's letters to Roy reveal him as an active and affectionate uncle: invitations to stay, advice on Roy's education and career, involving Roy in the life of his family and cousins in the South. I don't remember ever having a conversation with him about planning my life. He would wave a hand and say, 'fine, fine.' By that time however, a decade or more later, he was burdened by stresses unthought of during the years of village life.

Donald revived the Ingatestone cricket club. He organised an annual cricket match between the village and *The Times*. I loved these August Bank Holiday events, cucumber sandwiches and orange squash and climbing up onto the huge grass-roller. The cricket pitch is at the far side of the village green, just above the railway cutting. Whenever I go past in a train to Suffolk, I salute the pavilion.

The years of daily commuting to his long-hours job on *The Times*, plus the night-time wakefulness of young children, were taking their toll on Donald, and the family reluctantly moved back to London in the summer of 1951. A friend found a flat on Euston Road near Regent's Park. Donald was tied up at work and anyway couldn't drive or pace round likely locations. Margaret was occupied with four young children, my brother Robert just a few months old. The strain on her during these months resulted in mastitis and a return to hospital together with the baby. After the house and garden in the village, the urban flat, though spacious, was a disconnected cage for them up on the sixth floor. Not at all the kind of place they imagined for themselves.

Margaret had to adjust to the limitations of her new life. Just as the family was growing she had a feeling of loss. The move to London was the end of her public life. A second fledgling career cut short. She would never again enjoy the active collaboration with Donald, political, intellectual and social, that had begun in Southampton. When Donald was appointed Editor of the *Economist* in 1955, among the letters of congratulation was one from Joss Barnes, an old school friend from the North East, then based at RAF Stanmore. He asked after Margaret. 'Is she still doing great things in the local government arena?' I wonder how my mother felt when she read this, already a long way from that life? Living nearer Donald's office didn't seem to make much difference. Both of them had less freedom in the city than they'd had in the village. In August, we had our first holiday in Suffolk, seeding a life-long commitment to East Anglia which over the years represented my father's escape from urban confinement.

In September we were taken to the fairgrounds of the Festival of Britain. To the helter-skelter in Battersea Park and the Skylon balancing in the air outside the Festival Hall on the South Bank by Waterloo. Years later, my father took me to the Robert Mayer children's concerts in the Royal Festival Hall on Saturday mornings. We rode up to the auditorium in a lift shared with harps and double basses.

The festival mood fed into October's General Election. People were tired of austerity and voted the Conservatives back into power. This was the beginning of the end of the post-war consensus and my parents' youthful idealism. It was also the start of cold-war fears over the atomic bomb. The year 1951 was dubbed the 'Whose finger on the trigger?' election. Further, just as my father weathered the upheaval intended to ease his life on a daily paper, there was mounting tension in *The Times* office over who would succeed William Casey as Editor. The exhilaration of his appointment as Assistant Editor in 1944 soon gave way to unbearable suspense.

How oblivious I was to what happened in 1951. I certainly didn't understand how the 'wild rages' and dawn waking of three small girls added to the exhaustion my father felt in his daily commute. I do remember the large flat we moved into on the Euston Road, a row of sedate rooms at the front and a clutch of smaller rooms up the corridor. I remember playing in the broad hallway, Dad writing in his study, Aunty Spot staying to help with us three girls when my mother was in hospital with newborn Robert. I remember the delight of having a key to the gardens nearby and running back and forth through the scary tunnel under the main road.

Printing House Square

It was hard for Donald to leave the *Economist* and the *Observer* but on neither paper did he have full editorial control and the lure of Printing House Square was irresistible. The influence of *The Times* in those days was so great that people often conflated its views with that of Government. Negotiations between the *Economist*, the *Observer* and *The Times* took a while. There was regret and praise. Tom Jones wrote to Donald:

> Of course I am desperately sorry from the *Observer* angle...
> but I recognise that an invitation from *The Times* does not
> come every day... I should like to join Lord Astor and David
> in saying how much we have valued the quality and quantity of
> work you have put into the paper. It had supplied the backbone
> which it needed.

THESE ARE SOME OF TH[ ]EADER-WRITERS

THE TIMES: DONALD TYERMAN

The great newspaper of traditional conservatism, now distinguished by its courageous independence. Its staff includes Donald Tyerman, better known as a broadcaster on economics. Educated at Brasenose College, Oxford, a former lecturer in history at Southampton, he joined the "Economist" in 1937, and became acting editor in 1940, writing 9,000 words a week for four years. In 1943, was deputy editor of the "Observer." Joined "The Times" last October. An outstanding figure among younger journalists

DAILY MIRROR: BERNARD BUCKHAM

Most vigorous left-wing paper. Sixty-three-year-old Bernard Buckham ("B.B.B.") educated at Ipswich, worked on the "Daily Sketch" and the "Evening Standard" before he became London editor of the "Daily Dispatch," editor of the "Sunday Herald" (1916-20). His stories and sketches have appeared in the periodical press, and he describes his favourite recreation as "building castles in the air." His no-nonsense leaders are directed towards a mass of readers who know what they want (e.g. on houses)

DAILY TELEGRAPH: CAPT. C. R. COOTE

The solidly Conservative paper. Among its leader-writers (including H. C. Bailey and Malcolm Muggeridge) is Capt. Coote, educated at Rugby and Balliol College, Oxford. He served in the 1914-18 war, received the D.S.O. in 1918. Between 1917 and 1922, he was the Coalition Liberal M.P. for the Isle of Ely. He has written two books on Italy. For some years he was "The Times" correspondent in Rome, but when Geoffrey Dawson left that newspaper, Capt. Coote joined the "Daily Telegraph"

NEWS CHRONICLE: HUBERT PHILLIPS

The Liberal paper. Hubert Phillips is 54, was educated at Merton College, Oxford, where he took a first in modern history and a diploma in economics and political science. At 28, he became head of the economics department at Bristol. He gave up teaching and politics to join the "News Chronicle" in 1930. Started the Dogberry column and has been bridge editor and crossword editor. Has produced forty books. They include satirical verse, fiction, puzzles, works on politics, economics and bridge

DAILY HERALD: PERCY CUDLIPP

Official Labour paper, now free to express its unfettered Socialist views. At 40, Cudlipp is the youngest editor of a national morning newspaper and the only editor who also writes leaders. He has held the chair for five years. Educated at Cardiff, Cudlipp was dramatic critic and humorous columnist on the "Sunday News," which he left to become special writer and film critic on the "Evening Standard" (1929-31). He was promoted to be assistant editor in 1931, and editor in 1933, when he was only 28

DAILY MAIL: GEORGE MURRAY

The paper of vigorous Toryism. After two years in the Merchant Navy, George Murray submitted political verse to Fleet Street in 1920 but failed to get a job there. Spent seven years in the provinces, was then a reporter on the "Sunday Dispatch." During this war, he broadcast a weekly commentary on the N. American service. Murray has written about 2,000 editorials since he joined the "Daily Mail." Hits hard for the Government but his paper nowadays is often Liberal-minded (e.g. on Beveridge)

The post-war leader-writers, *Leader* magazine, 1945

The Times Editor, Robin Barrington-Ward, signalled in his letters to Donald that there would be 'no limits' to Donald's progress on the paper. Here was the informal promise of the editorship that dogged the whole of Donald's period on the paper. As with his position on both the weeklies, once again there would be responsibility without power. I was beginning to see how central a characteristic this was of my father's professional life. Proprietors and colleagues trusted him with the unremitting core job of editing and producing papers but always withheld true independence. Barrington-Ward did mean it, however, and things might have been different if he himself had not died only four years after Donald's appointment. But in 1944, he wanted Donald to join him as soon as possible for 'a long, happy and progressive association'.

The inside story of Donald's years at *The Times* is revealed in a long but intermittent correspondence with Stanley Morison, a First World War conscientious objector and Roman Catholic convert, who became a consultant on *The Times* from 1929, was Editor of *The Times Literary Supplement* from 1945–48 and became official historian of the paper in the fifties. He was the inventor of the 'Times New Roman' font I often type with, introduced in 1932 after criticisms of the paper's ageing appearance. Donald was thirty-six in 1944. Morison was sixty-six. Donald wrote in green or black ink on small cards with *The Times* letterhead or in large, scrawling pencil on plain notepaper. He wrote late at night or over the weekend.

Stanley Morison had supported Donald's appointment to *The Times* and support was what Donald continued to expect. His choice of confidante was distinctly unwise. John Pringle, a foreign correspondent who came to *The Times* in 1948 from the *Manchester*

Guardian and the BBC, and who was Donald's friend as well as colleague, described Morison as a born intriguer who had the ear of *Times* Chief Proprietor Lord Astor and others after hours at the Garrick Club, a man who in fact disapproved of Donald for being 'infected by liberalism' and, together with the paper's Board of Directors (chaired by Lord Astor), saw Donald as 'some kind of alien'.

Donald intended to stay at *The Times* long term, though even he was aware of personal and cultural barriers to his advancement:

> I don't think I shall ever be the Editor of T.T. because I lack the social competence and social inclination (both conflicting as they do with my determination to be independent, as a person, as a villager and as a family man, against all the horrid and hideous attractions of London life). I might consider one of the few independent editorships but it is most unlikely that they would be offered to me. I expect to stay at P.H.S. until pension-time.

He confided to Morison the personal root of his desire for an independence that he also knew was elusive:

> Since I lay disabled on my back when a child and a youth, my ambition has been (a) to be independent (which seemed unlikely but which has been accomplished) and (b) in particular to be 'an Editor'. Thus I look at my future. I want to be an independent Editor (almost all Editors, and all the best paid ones, are <u>not</u> independent).

Editorial meeting, *The Times*, 1946

Donald's wood-panelled room in Printing House Square (PHS) was dark and lamp-lit. The bookshelves were high and the furniture heavy, including a large conference table. From his desk, Donald undertook a huge amount and variety of work, starting with a bold attack on Churchill for his policy of intervention against the partisans in Greece. Donald wrote and edited articles on Germany, Europe, the welfare state, London, New Towns and Garden Cities. It quickly became clear to him that the post-war *Times* was not in good shape. There was a serious shortage of leader-writers, there were no explicit procedures for decisions on staffing or finances, there were internal conflicts and rivalries, office culture was narrow and arrogant. Donald began sending memos to try and sort things out. The lack of response was draining. Writing in confidence to

E.H. Carr, historian and colleague who was about to leave the paper to write books full-time, Donald responds in detail to questions about the editorial side of the paper, specifically the difficulty of appointing a new assistant editor, an economics leader-writer and a foreign leader-writer to succeed Carr. He identifies four obstacles:

> First, it is an attribute of the Editor's great personal qualities that he is allergic to organisation. Secondly, the Manager is allergic to expenditure, which is the dominating factor throughout the present set-up. Thirdly, nothing can clearly be defined as regards the functions or prospects of possible recruits... Fourthly, an important obstacle is the present set-up itself, and personalities...there is an astonishing weakness on the leader-writing side, which is I admit covered up with reasonable success but only by quite laborious improvisation... We do manage to rub along sufficiently well but not for the near distant future, when peacetime and competitive journalism is likely to return to find the effective editorial side of P.H.S. manned by a tiny and somewhat confused skeleton staff.

Donald is forthright and thorough in his criticism of the running of the paper, which he finds to be lazy, opaque and complacent. He is seriously disappointed. On 17 January 1947 Donald spelled out to Morison what had changed since his appointment in 1944:

> I had in mind (a) the professional advantage and (b) the fact that I could work with B.W. in ideas and presentation (I was right). Now there is a difference. Barrington-Ward was ill, E.H. Carr had left, other writers had come. (a) was up but (b) was

down, which puts a premium in my mind on the institutional frustration and friction which are occupational ailments here at P.H.S. Heaven knows I have no claim to the Editorship, the biggest job on earth, but I have a view on T.T. as a climate of work and ideas. On that view I made my decision to come. On that view, revised, I will make my decision to stay. That's all. I'm really very humble. I'm a good servant. But I have my own ideals, such as they are, to serve. Hence my doubtings. Not pride, but simple anxiety. Just a common newspaperman, with no false pretensions – but with a very clear view of T.T. as it should be, I think.

Reform was even more urgent than three years before. Donald strains to take proper responsibility and feel energised to do his professional best, though from a position of humility. He goes forward and he holds back.

A memo about Home News and Night Staff of 3 February 1947, circulated confidentially to senior staff ahead of a discussion with the editor, sets out what's wrong:

The paper is not succeeding as a <u>news</u>-paper on the home side because of the shortage of space, material that is carried for the record but which is not really news, chronic under-staffing especially in the evening and at night, with poor liaising between night and day staff, too few people doing too many jobs while no one has sufficient time or authority to plan or to think. So the night editions are not taken seriously at all, which means that readers get a paper deficient in home news and probably grossly out-of-date compared with competitors because of our deliberate policy of printing too many of the middle editions. Playing it safe is symptomatic and, as I see it, most damaging.

I feel the frustration mounting behind this analysis, Donald controlling himself to spell out the paper's glaring flaws but receiving little or no response. In the summer of 1947, Geoffrey Crowther made an approach to Donald about returning to the *Economist* but after discussing it all with Margaret, 'who matters most', he said 'No'.

On 1 March 1948, Donald's fortieth birthday, Robin Barrington-Ward died. This was sudden, though not unexpected, as his health had been poor for some time, compounded by overwork. Two days later Donald wrote to Morison: 'if I'm not picked now. I never will be'. Colleague John Pringle remembered that 'there were weeks of ludicrous intrigue and hesitation which was particularly unfair on Tyerman, who through all this period had had to carry the burden of actually editing the paper.' Donald was left for days on end in sole charge of getting the paper out but without recognition or security. The board could not agree between 'the two outstanding candidates', one of whom was Donald. They finally appointed William Casey, who had joined the paper in 1913 as a sports writer and was intending to retire in a year's time. Donald was made Deputy Editor. On 3 April, the *Evening Standard's* 'Londoner's Diary' declared that Donald's 'new work seems to mark him out as Casey's successor'. This was the view from outside. The inside view was described by John Pringle in his memoir *Have Pen Will Travel*:

Some of the directors thought that, for all his obvious strength, ability and power of decision, Donald Tyerman, who came from a grammar school background [this was not the case –

he came from a municipal secondary school] in the north of England and was a cripple as the result of poliomyelitis as a child, was somehow too 'uncouth' to be editor of *The Times*. One of them even invited him to dinner to observe his clothes and table manners – and then rang him to let him know his conclusions.

Margaret also observed the prejudices:

We lived near Regent's Park and one Sunday he went round Regent's Park in his chair and he met one of the directors who wrote to somebody and said that it wouldn't be dignified to have the editor going about in a wheelchair.

The Times director who was repelled by the sight of Donald riding round the park was Sir Campbell Stuart, Canadian newspaperman, Knight Commander of the Most Excellent Order of the British Empire and veteran of the Second World War Special Operations Executive.

On 1 March 1949, Donald's birthday once again, and one year on from the death of Barrington-Ward, Donald wrote:

I'll be 41 tomorrow (Tuesday), older and wiser – and still sadder for the worst personal loss I've had since I joined this trade. It's been a bad twelve months, with my oldest and best Oxford friend and mentor – Stallybrass [Principal of Brasenose College in the 1920s] – gone as well as B.W. – and there's something odd and eerie in these January-February days with another Editor away sick, as B.W. was last year.

By 1951, Donald's letters to Morison increased, their tone often bitter as the uncertainty and suspense over Casey's successor deepened. 'I won't stay,' he wrote.

> My ambition has been to run my own show before I'm old. If it can't be T.T. – and this well may be the decision – then the *Ipswich Journal* or the *King's Lynn Courier*. Until the time for a decision comes I'm *The Times*'s, bodily and mentally, as now. But there's not enough virtue in London or even P.H.S. to justify my being No 2 for a quarter of a century.

On 1 August, Donald wrote a five-page letter to Morison – small black handwriting scrupulously legible as always – from the Swan Hotel in Southwold, Suffolk, where we were staying for our first family holiday since the move from Essex to London. I remember the wet and the wind as we children trailed with my mother along to the Dutch Barn café on the path to the harbour, waves crashing close on the beach in that pre-Flood summer, the marram-grass dyke not yet built. Donald was in the hotel, staring out at the rain.

He feels his gruelling work amounts to 'taking in washing', that's all the value given to it by colleagues and senior managers. Donald writes to Morison because he's the only one left alive from those who appointed him to *The Times*. His tone is 'stiff' because they haven't been in touch for two years or more. Donald reminds Morison that it's only for his eyes. Casey had told him in January that he was staying on indefinitely and also the Chairman Lord Astor, 'whose remoteness from the paper and what really goes on there is only exceeded by his remoteness from me'. Donald couldn't talk to either of them. He regrets moving from the *Economist* and

The Observer and he regrets saying 'No' to Crowther in 1946. He senses his own value falling, with age and the failure of the promises initially made to him at *The Times*:

All the possibilities which I discovered in myself between 1941 and 1944 at the *Economist* and at *The Observer* have been lodged in me useless all these years while I have become a super-wicket-keeper or, better, perhaps, a caretaker of skill, discretion and industry. Maybe if I had followed the gleam of my capabilities I would have disappointed myself but within the requirements of T.T. I haven't even tried. The promise has rusted. How ordinary the paper is, though its merits are high, and how good, even thrilling we could make it!

Me with my mother and father, Southwold, 1951

The 'grand' holiday by the sea was a vital escape.

On 18 August Donald wrote to Morison that the previous two years had been 'bizarre'. The consequences of a heavy workload were serious, being tied to the office means being out of the loop of talk in clubland. He passes on gossip that colleagues are peddling about Morison's disloyalty:

> Continuous ties in the office have withdrawn me from outside contacts, personal and public, which were once many and wide – and the loss may now be a real liability. I am absent from the many discussions of T.T. which always go on wherever men talk, so that it is only now, when lately I have had a few free days, that I am told, by good men though I don't know on what authority, that men are being approached to be editor of T.T. and, with reluctance but by more than one, that S.M. is no friend of mine in these affairs.

Margaret believed that Donald's unquestioning trust in others was the result of his immobility: 'He could never imagine why anyone would be unkind to him. I think partly through being lame that he didn't have quite so much of the rough and tumble.' My father's immobility gave rise to all sorts of other exclusions, social and emotional as well as physical. This is a powerfully clear dimension of my father's experience of life but one I never appreciated, growing up. Whatever he was in the life I shared with him was, of course, normal.

Donald goes over and over earlier conversations with Morison, trying to work out what the recent discussions might mean, asking why he hadn't kept his promise to tell Donald if the chance of promotion really had gone.

We have, I know not why, drifted apart; it is over two years since we met for a meal or to talk at your initiative. If there are oddities about this letter excuse them by my utter loneliness, by the fact that there has been literally no-one with whom I could talk openly and honestly during these years when I have gone on month after month with the job. I have been literally dumb, bottled up and perhaps now may have it distorted – though I don't think so. I don't know why I should apologise again, though. I have nothing to apologise for. You in all this have seemed to me, however distant, the good man.

Morison rang as soon as he received the letter but Donald was in the bath:

I tried to ring you when I clambered out of my bath on Saturday but I could not get through. I had to dash off with my daughter Anne for a day in the country and when I got back full of sunshine and pleasant memories of country cricket and smiling fields I could not bring myself to think of anything remotely connected with P.H.S. Today I am in harness again on the job of putting the paper together out of practically nothing, which has taken all my time. I want to assure you that I did not want to be rude in not replying to your prompt call.

Producing the paper day by day is a 'conjuring trick', Donald writes bitterly. In his next letter to Morison, he indicates the extent of malicious gossip:

129

I have been pondering words of yours. Did you mean to imply that I'd be a better man if I went more to theatres et al., and that in default of this there is a defect in me? If so, I'm put out. I am by nature an inveterate theatre-goer et al, just as I'm an inveterate games watcher. I don't do these things, or haven't done during the past two years or so because I haven't had the time or the opportunity. I am preaching no indispensability here at P.H.S., it's mostly the routine of the job, the scissors and paste, that tie me, but tied I have been during the fatigue, sickness, ill-health, absence and the rest, of editors and Deputies… I'm not such a dull dog or clod as you clubmen might suppose. Someday I'll frolic and take the right cultured waters (non-alcoholic) but meanwhile don't scold me for not being frolicsome. But I've a sense of duty made twice as big by watching B.W.'s sacrifice and trying to stave it off.

Ironic wit conveys my father's exhaustion and isolation. Even after so long the burden of his angry self-defence against class prejudice and professional inertia is painful to read.

In 1952, the succession was finally resolved. Here was the final blow to Donald's expectations. Sir William Haley, Director General of the BBC since 1944, was appointed Editor. In his diaries Haley describes my father as a 'first class journalist' whose departure from the paper 'would be a severe loss'. He hopes Donald will stay on but he makes it clear he wants Donald himself to decide what's best for his future career. Haley describes Donald as both 'reserved' and 'restless'. He acknowledges Donald's huge workload and responsibility during the last years as Deputy Editor. *Times* board members of an older generation had always been dismissive towards

Donald. Sir Campbell Stuart, who'd been so disturbed by the sight of Donald riding his three-wheeler round Regent's Park, urges Haley to 'stop making a fuss about Tyerman'.

Haley's diaries reveal how much manoeuvring went on in the clubland lunches and dinners where professional and social networks intertwined and where strategic words in certain ears carried enormous weight. Donald was largely excluded from this Establishment scene, where negative gossip circulated unchecked. Once he was stung enough to write to Haley:

> I never take notice of what people say about me in other sheets. I'm sure you don't either. But I do wince when my personal relations and special friends and colleagues, such as I hope and believe, indeed know, you are, are brought into the tale… I have resented deeply the suggestion that our relations were based on anything but trust, loyalty and a friendship that I value. What anyone thinks of me doesn't matter…but the idea that I was the fly in your ointment and the source of your unease…seems to me outrageous. I look back with pride and pleasure and gratitude to our happy and productive time at PHS.

The lunches Donald himself organised were often gatherings of potential recruits to the paper, young writers with whom he felt at ease, ever the facilitating mentor.

Sir William Haley fitted the Board of Directors' vision of a public figure commensurate with the editorship. His first job as a young man had been on *The Times*. At the BBC he inaugurated the annual Reith Lectures in 1948 and set up the Third Programme. Now he was ready to leave, partly because the Conservative Government indicated their support for commercial television, heralding unwelcome changes in broadcasting. But if the Board looked forward to a grandee as Editor, the day-today reality was rather different.

John Midgley, Donald's long-term friend and colleague on both *The Times* and the *Economist* said:

> They didn't know what they were doing because William Haley, although it was true he was Director General of the BBC and a KCMG, on paper and to their eyes a distinguished public figure, what he really was was a working journalist and he came to *The Times* and took off his coat and rolled up his shirt sleeves. I'm not saying the decision to have Haley was wrong, though I think the decision to prefer Haley to Tyerman was wrong. Journalistically, Tyerman would have done a better job. The idea that you would have Haley instead of Tyerman for the reason that Haley was a man of public dignity was absolutely idiotic.

Rolling your sleeves up and getting on with the job were obviously good for the paper, a professional approach that Haley and Donald shared, though I can see that the shy and high-minded Haley, experienced manager of another, much larger, unique British institution, could be tougher and more decisive than my father. Despite Donald's great disappointment, Donald and William Haley became friends. When Donald was preparing to leave Printing House Square to take up the editorship of the *Economist* in 1955, he wrote:

> My dear WSH, I cannot let you go on holiday without saying, however awkwardly, how very deeply I will regret the parting

and how very much I have valued, personally and professionally, being with you… What you have already done for and with *The Times* in shaping a fine and worthy chapter in the story. Thank you. Yours, DT

They always exchanged books at Christmas.

The letters from Donald to Stanley Morison chart a professional and emotional struggle that, despite the promises, he was never going to win. They are as intimate, in their way, as the letter to my mother before they married. They reveal the tensions that were integral to his character and of which he was well aware. His desire to be independent but collaborative and his love of an institution that would never return his embrace both contributed to a second form of paralysis. Donald was never going to be 'one of us' in Printing House Square, with his modernising and progressive tendencies, his home-knitted jumpers underneath a suit jacket, his distasteful disability, his innocence of implicit codes of behaviour, his annoying neediness, the very contradiction of ambitious humility underlined by the refusal to assert his ego.

Perhaps Donald's misguided choice of confidante didn't matter in the end. The letters read like monologues. Donald was writing for himself. There was no colleague he could talk to nor, as the family grew during the 1940s and 1950s, could there be hours of stressful late-night discussion with Margaret at home. At least, this is what I have assumed. Now I wonder if it would have been too much for my mother and that she signalled this, cutting off his chance to let off steam because she feared being flattened by it herself. Their worlds were separating fast. Donald needed to get all his thoughts and feelings out, so he substituted writing to Morison for these impossible conversations with his wife. His pencil dug into the rough paper with dark verticals. The letters go inside Donald Tyerman as well as inside *The Times*.

Donald was appointed Editor of the *Economist* in the autumn of 1955 and returned to the orbit of Geoffrey Crowther. Hundreds of letters of congratulation arrived from Britain, Europe, America and Africa The contrast between this correspondence and the anguished letters Donald wrote to Stanley Morison is stunning. People with famously opposite political and personal views wrote with the same admiration and affection: historians, business leaders, industrialists, diplomats, civil servants, lawyers, and publishers, as well as family, friends, ex-students and fellow-journalists in Fleet Street and broadcasting.

Fleet Street colleagues echoed the comments made in the press when Donald was appointed to *The Times* in 1944. They were proud to know him. He was still one of the most remarkable figures in journalism. They never doubted such an appointment would come. Many had expected him to be made Editor of *The Times* and regretted this hadn't happened. Others referred explicitly to the difficulties Donald had faced in Printing House Square and regarded his move to the *Economist* as a calamity for *The Times*. One said he would miss the sight of his 'steadfast blunt pencil and rueful grin' as he edited leader copy late at night.

Valediction
A valedictory dinner was held at Printing House Square in December 1955. Official photographs show that at each of two round tables decorated with flowers and silver candelabras were seated eight men

and two women, the cutlery laid for the beginning of the meal. The room is panelled, with tapestry curtains, a marble fireplace and portraits. Donald is looking at the camera, dark eyes full of thought. Margaret, on the other table, is looking down. The men on her right and left are not speaking to her. I don't recognise her black dress or her hairstyle, parted and held at the back. She looks young, elegant and shy.

One photograph shows Donald and William Haley shaking hands. They are both smiling. Donald wears his Brasenose College tie. Haley has presented Donald with a black leather autograph book. The cover has a gold border with 'DT' stamped in gold in the centre. The book contains 184 signatures. Donald holds this in his left hand, resting it firmly on the edge of the table to steady himself. Another photo shows Donald speaking. He is standing up, one hand on the table with fingers bent, the other gripping the arm of his chair. Haley and Gavin Astor sit to his left. An illustrious forebear hangs in a golden frame on the wall behind them.

Donald begins his speech by giving thanks. He's self-deprecating, he's only been in Printing House Square for eleven years, so it's not a special departure, he's not even retiring. He had never before worked on a daily paper. His tenure has been 'irregular'. He tells his audience what went right, and what went wrong, too – this added in the margin of his notes as a corrective afterthought – so like him, in form as well as in content. Donald remembered arriving at the paper during the last stages of the war. Then came the Labour government, Bernadotte, the Czech Coup, the fuel crisis, strikes. And SPORT [his capitals]: 'THIS I WILL MISS'. 'FRIENDSHIP is the 'ESSENTIAL THING', also 'PRIDE IN 'TT' and 'ACHIEVEMENT TOGETHER', my father's beloved collective anonymity, 'THE JOB'S THE THING'.

Donald, who joined the paper one April, described himself as a cuckoo. How true, I thought. Yet, he went on, the cuckoo who belonged, 'always'. Not true I thought. How could he have felt that he belonged, after all he suffered and all the ways in which he clearly was used, relied on but excluded? Donald loved and revered the institution itself and what the paper could be, despite his personal disappointments, and he was always sentimental about the friendship of colleagues. 'The Cuckoo That Belonged' was Donald's wishful Just-So Story.

The cuckoo was a *Times* in-joke, of course, coming from the fantasy gardens of rural clergymen taking the air before settling down to write next Sunday's sermon. The song of the first cuckoo in spring was originally, though as it turned out mistakenly, celebrated in a letter published in February 1913:

> While gardening this afternoon I heard a faint note, which led me to say to my under-gardener, who was working with me, 'Was that the cuckoo?' Almost immediately afterwards we both heard the full double note of a cuckoo, repeated either two or three times. There is not the slightest doubt that the song was that of a cuckoo. (Rev. R. Lydekker, Harpenden Lodge. Hertfordshire)

It was a bricklayer's labourer whistling. The real thing mattered, though. A *Times* editorial of 22 February 1913, entitled 'The Delight of April', declared that 'the voice of the cuckoo seems to fall from the sky like a celestial encouragement to all… There is no other time when the senses are all so harmoniously enchanted.'

Family Life: the house

After living in the flat on Marylebone Road for a year, we moved to a large and draughty house in Parsifal Road, West Hampstead, described by Pevsner as 'Victorian red brick at its worst'. My father's armchair was in the sitting room, which had French windows on to the garden. We ran in and out as he cried 'Shut the bloody door!'

To my 1950s London street came the onion-seller from 'France' with ropes of vegetables hanging off his handlebars, the rag-and-bone man with his cart and his bell, and the knife-grinder with his sewing-machine treadle, throwing out sparks to a shrill whine from the blades. There was smog: damp and tangy, white but black in its effects, impenetrable and enticing. Coal was delivered in canvas sacks worn shiny by time. The men wore leather overalls and stained gauntlets. There was thunder as the lumps fell down the chute into the cellar, filling the air with metallic dust.

Before Hendon Way became the slip road to the M1, Finchley Road was an avenue lined with plane trees and huge villas behind front gardens. On the corner with Parsifal Road lived Mr Edwards, alone and beyond age in his decaying fortress, a bogey-man to race past on the way to the newsagent. Though there was hardly any traffic up or down the steep road, we stayed on the pavement. Hopscotch on the flagstones: a grid of squares drawn in chalk and a stone to drop on the right one. That was the skill and the luck, no-go if you miss. Then hopping, jumping and turning. We could easily have kicked a ball in the street but we didn't kick balls, we threw them and caught them, hit them and bounced them, against the side of the theological college at the top of the hill or the kitchen wall in the back garden. One of our games was a ten-down-to-one sequence of increasingly hard tricks with a tennis ball in which you lose the turn if it falls to the ground. Or we skipped with a heavy washing line if there were at least three of us, two to hold and swing the ends. Timing was everything. It wasn't how high you could jump or how closely you watched the spin of the rope. The beat was what mattered.

I went to Brownies in Beckford School, round the corner in Mill Lane. I was a Fairy, bright and gay, helping others every day. I enjoyed the singing and dancing and was not much affected by the patriotic and evangelical ethos. The point of being a Brownie was being allowed out on my own at night. To buy chips in Fortune Green Road on the way home. There was no way I could go on to be a Guide. That would involve 'Flying up', passing like a Pilgrim to the 'other side', that is, the end of the Hall and the end of your childhood. Two Guides would be waiting to lift me off the ground. I could not imagine any of that.

The first celebration of our new life in NW6 was the christening party for my youngest brother Christopher, born in May 1953. It was warm enough to be out in the garden. Photographs show friends and family, dressed up in a scruffy space. Round the edge were flower beds with hollyhocks, lupins and foxgloves. Dog roses hung over the fence. Irises grew in the front garden. A wooden hut at the far end of the back garden was a playhouse for a while but it soon became too decrepit for the simplest games. My father would sit on the bench and bowl at us, batting from the apple tree wicket.

On Saturday mornings, the first one up would go down to the front door to collect the newspapers and hand them over to my father, still in bed. As he would read anything and everything within reach, we had to be quick to retrieve our comics or he'd play-act total absorption in *The Beano*'s Bash Street Kids or Dan Dare in *The Eagle*. This magazine once ran a story about a detective who directed operations from his Iron Lung, polio again topical due to the epidemic of the late 1950s.

My father always got up after us. He had to take his time and he had his rituals. The bathroom had several stools and laundry boxes that he used to navigate his way across the room and into and out of the bath. His arms were hugely strong and he was able to lift himself from place to place without any help. He remembered being carried for the first ten years or so of his life. He feared a return to this dependence more than anything.

The bathroom was at the end of the landing, with a separate lavatory next door. I remember having baths with my younger sister, Mary. One game involved putting the wooden soap rack across the bath between us and filling it with the tubes, tins and bottles that sat around the ledges. Then we would mix them all up, cooking a stew that we called 'galosha'. Our saucepan was the shallow tin that the toothpaste came in. This was a pink cakey substance, easily reduced to liquid to absorb the other ingredients.

Bakelite telephones were black and heavy, the earpiece and mouthpiece attached to the base by an ox-blood cord of plaited wire. There was one on a shelf at shoulder height in the hall and one on a side table in the dining room, where prints of a Cezanne *Montagne Sainte-Victoire* (1887) and a Van Gogh *Wheatfield with Cypresses* (1889) hung on the panelled walls (1882). During the week this room was mine. I had a squad of oil heaters to arrange round my chair. Here I did my homework, practised Mendelssohn on the rickety piano, listened to records (Bach, Tchaikovsky, Flanders and Swann, Adam Faith) and spoke at length on the phone to friends I had been with all day. In the late afternoons I sat by the window and dragged my index finger round the telephone's chrome dial, waiting impatiently as it came back to rest between each letter and digit. Our number was HAM 1030. It was necessary to dissect every happening and conversation, all overhearings and significant sightings, to explore every nuance and to share in detail our deepest loves and hates, winding down from the dramas, putting off the history essay or the French translation. We could talk for as long as we liked for 4 old pence.

In the room next door, my father sat, reading or writing, and after 1956 watching the television set that was a leaving present from *The Times*. *Andy Pandy*, *Muffin the Mule*, *In Town Tonight*, *Panorama*, these were my first programmes. We had crumpets as we watched *Grandstand* on Saturday afternoons. I can still hear the long roll-call of match results, that inflected voice, up for the first team, down for the second, and Rugby League's unforgettable 'Hulking Stone Rovers'. I don't remember my father using the phone at all.

He would have to be sitting right by it. There was a bedside extension upstairs. He couldn't stand up and speak into the one in the hall and he couldn't just wander into the dining room for a chat with a friend or colleague. All his talking was face-to-face. Hardly any of that at home. Maybe more than enough of that at work.

Before London went smokeless, Dad sat by the hearth, legs out in front, holding a newspaper against the grate to channel air. He had only three domestic chores. As well as keeping the fire going, he had to sew on his own buttons and he had to wrap Christmas presents. When string gave way to Sellotape, he became entangled and enraged. How he would have loved hi-tech. Imagine if he could have slipped a smartphone in his pocket, thousands of books, international news updates, podcasts, films, music and a surfeit of talk. He would have been exasperated when his broad fingers tapped the wrong icon. He would have chucked the wretched thing across the room. Yet I can hear his 'Aha!' as he accessed today's e-book or blog. He would be firing off text messages to the rest of us in our separate rooms, filling and crossing 3-D space with running-gags of virtual humour. Tweeting would have been irresistible. What a feeling of movement it would have given him, however eye-rolling it would be for my mother, sighing for a bit of peace in the kitchen. And for me, diverted away from my Bach Prelude or the landline, themselves diversions from the *Gallic Wars* or *Lettres de Mon Moulin*. I can see my father Skyping friends and family, in the North and overseas, once he'd got the hang of it, once he'd relaxed into a post-work, post-aperitivo *bonhomie*, time-zone slippage quite forgotten. He would have been demanding, irritating, amusing, in the way, involved. More like the sort of father who could tramp round the house any time he liked.

Dad bowling at my brothers, London, 1959

Coastal Strip Theory

Childhood Augusts were spent in Walberswick, Suffolk. Our new London GP's aunt-in-law owned a bungalow right by the dunes. For more than a decade the seven of us, plus Magic the cat and Pickle the dog (in honour of his Essex predecessor), squashed into Morris Oxford Traveller, LBW 812 (Leg Before Wicket for cricket fans, transferred from car to car), and drove to the east coast: down to Golders Green, turn right at Henly's Corner onto the North Circular, past Shadbolt's timber yard by the Lea at Edmonton and onto the A12. My father always called it 'A12'. He never said 'the A12'. Then he would intone his Coastal Strip Theory. This states that any weather forecast is irrelevant for the strip of land between 'A12' and the sea.

It was a long way from London in those days. Ozone meant freedom. We were not allowed to cycle in London. 'It's too dangerous,' said my mother. Her unspoken reason was that if she set a cut-off point of a specific age, blood would soon flow across that divide and the noise would be unbearable. I see her point though I think she was wrong and I wish she'd sorted out a system. No wonder I was envious of my school-friends who cycled every day from Maida Vale up to Swiss Cottage. When I began cycling in London thirty years later, defying that old prohibition still gave me pleasure.

I did ride a bike in Suffolk. We hired them from Old Mr Richards and Young Mr Richards. Their garage-shop was behind the petrol pump at the bottom of the village green, where we also bought fishing lines to go crabbing on the Kissing Bridge over the creek by the harbour. Young Mr Richards was tall and stooped. He must have been over seventy. Bikes were how I got about, exploring places and friendships without supervision or sibling irritations. I hardly remember going back for meals, maybe egg-bread for breakfast, but what we ate for supper, I couldn't tell you. I can still feel the swish of wheels as I hurtled down between two cottages, feet off the pedals to turn sharp right with a scrunch into the lane by our summer home. I smell wet clothes not-drying in front of a gas fire.

The magnet for me on holiday was the riding stables. It was a wrench to go as far as the common for a picnic or to the beach for a swim, though I did love the sea. There was a sizeable village green with swings and a see-saw that made a great vantage point to check comings and goings, watching my father scull about on his chair, or my mother walk the dog, but the gravelly courtyard of the Anchor Inn was the hub. The noise and smelly disruption caused by the horses, grooms, riders and swarming hangers-on, only a few of whom were pub customers, caused ongoing friction with the landlord. When he wanted to convert the stables into a drinks store and build new chalets round the back, we had to go. Old Mr Cleminson, known as 'Clem', a gentleman whose age we could only guess at and who drove an open-topped car with a steering wheel on a long pole, offered the horses a new stable up the lane by the back of his house, on the other side of the main street. If I hear wood pigeons or smell pine, that is where I am.

I went out on rides with Mary or other stables regulars. A string of four or five of us went up onto the heath, as far as the old Halesworth-Southwold railway track alongside the Blyth estuary, which was really too soft and sandy for the horses, or south to the Heronry with its thin line of trees, then across the by-road before plunging round Hoist Covert for a final canter before cooling down on the walk back. Sometimes the blacksmith would be there, with his devilish grin, his eyes bright in a sooty face, stoking the embers of his fire, scraping the horses' hooves with a fine scimitar, hissing a new shoe in water before a first fitting, then banging it into shape on his anvil before leaning into the horse's backside to fix it with huge nails. I was entranced by the smell, the smoke and the percussion.

Getting up early to go and collect the horses from their overnight marshes was the most companionable, almost secret, delight. A group of us might cadge a lift from a volunteered parent to help carry the bridles but more often we walked, along the cool sandy tracks at the edge of the heath and the strip of road curling round to the river, pockets filled with stale bread and sugar lumps. Then it was riding bareback down into the village.

In the evenings I lurked in the back yard of the Bell pub, down by the harbour where the fishermen and the artists hung out, hoping for a Coke and crisps to be slipped out without the landlord noticing. I gossiped with friends I saw one month a year: Judith and Anna, willowy teenagers from west London, and blonde Jane with her salty laugh, who'd lived in the village all her life. I swam in the North Sea whatever the temperature and I walked on the chilly beach at night. I can still see Janet Alwood on the top of the dyke. During the day she worked as the official groom at the stables. But here she is, someone else entirely. Her cotton dress blows in the sunset breeze. She's walking her dog. She's a girl from a painting by Philip Wilson Steer, seventy years on. This is where she belongs.

Dad couldn't join us for the whole of August. He had to manage by himself in London. In the days when all messages were scrutinised by the village postmistress, he sent my mother a telegram: 'WHAT? NO TIN OPENER. HATE. DON.'

White City

Back in London, my father took us to the White City to watch athletics. Purpose-built in a hurry by local Hammersmith stonemason George Wimpey, the 1908 stadium was a late addition to the vast Franco-British Exhibition at Shepherd's Bush. Intended host country Italy withdrew after the major eruption of Vesuvius in 1906. New London tube and train lines were specially constructed. Joe Lyons provided the refreshments. These were the first Olympic Games to have a cinder running track and to fly national flags. There were demonstration events, like the gymnastic 'Danish Dianas' and cycle-polo. There's an eight-minute Pathé newsreel of these Games. Quick-fire sequences show pole-vaulting, the high jump, tugs of war, discus throwing and swimming in choppy water in a pool in the middle of the stadium while a peloton of bicycles flashes past on the track. At the end of the marathon, athletes leaned over and splashed water from the pool onto their faces and arms. The hats were terrific: Americans in white ten-gallon Stetsons, judges in bowlers and boaters, women archers with a whole bird's nest on their heads. Sir Arthur Conan Doyle reported on the Games for the *Daily Mail*. Announcements were made by foghorn.

We went to the '3As' at Whitsun, the Amateur Athletics Association meeting that functioned as the annual British Games. There were also two-way or three-way international meetings: Britain versus Hungary, Britain versus France versus Czechoslovakia. I was there in 1955 when Roger Bannister, Christopher Chataway and Chris Brasher reprised the smashing of the four-minute mile they first achieved the previous year in Oxford. I was there when Chataway beat Vladimir Kuts, 'the Leningrad sailor', to take 5 seconds off the 5000 metres world record he had secured only two months earlier at the European Championships in Berne. There was also Emil Zatopek, the Czech athlete who, in Prague only a few days later, pushed Kuts to a further world record.

There were no vast billboards or brand logos around the track. The only advertising was for the *News of the World*, the meetings' sponsor. There were loud-speaker announcements but no in-your-face trackside interviews with sweaty winners and losers, no roaring night-club music, no swathes of digitally enhanced images on huge screens, pulsating strobes of colour. There was no action-replay, no enhanced flat-screen imagery at all. There was no pretence that a middle-distance race was just like a muscle-bound sprint or that long-distance running did not in fact take ages but would, if allowed, draw you into a winding and subtle drama. The only other people who I know for sure will have switched off their phones at the time of a major international middle-distance race are my sisters.

My mother drove Dad and us girls across from West Hampstead, turning right into Iverson Road, across Kilburn High Road, along The Avenue to Willesden, then nearly to Wormwood Scrubs before turning left into Wood Lane. She did not come into the stadium. She went home and came back again. This was my father's special activity. Not much time off for my mother though, with the shuttling to and fro and the boys unstrapped in the back of the car.

My father twice rode his three-wheeler all the way to the White City. Once from the Marylebone Road and once from West Hampstead. Far less traffic in those pre-Westway days and he was still young, determined to get out on his own after the return to what my mother called the 'restrictions' of London. I can see him, flying along, face red with exertion, a flow and rhythm to the movement of his upper body, feeling free.

Ulysses

Two Men in a Lift

One day in the late 1950s two men shared a lift in a building near Blackfriars Bridge on the north bank of the Thames: Printing House Square (PHS), home of *The Times*. They were Donald Tyerman, the new editor of the *Economist*, and his predecessor, Geoffrey Crowther, who stayed on as Deputy Chairman of the *Economist* group. Neither of them was working for *The Times* so it was odd that they should be in Printing House Square at all, let alone on the same day. They were there because Donald had been asked to write Geoffrey's obituary and Geoffrey had been asked to write Donald's.

They first met that Christmas Eve in 1936 when Donald arrived at the *Economist* office in Bouverie Street for the job interview. Geoffrey was already on the staff. Donald was twenty-eight, Geoffrey twenty-nine. For more than thirty years they were significant figures in each other's life, especially from 1937–44, Donald's years as Assistant and often Acting Editor of the *Economist*, and from 1956–65, as Editor. Their long and dysfunctional relationship played out alongside my adolescence and was a source, I now realise, of the strained atmosphere at home.

Donald and Geoffrey both came from the North East of England and they shared important characteristics. Brilliant students, they each had a phenomenal photographic memory. For all their similarities, however, the two men in the lift that day were fundamentally different: Donald disabled but handsome, Geoffrey short and stout but charismatic. Geoffrey had dominated his siblings in their childhood nursery and would go on to be President of the Cambridge Union and, later, Chair of the Board of the *Economist*. He transformed the London skyline with the new *Economist* offices in St James's in the 1960s. From schooldays onwards Geoffrey was renowned for his sharp debating. Donald found him 'dazzling'. Both men loved sitting down in prestigious circumstances, but whereas Geoffrey would dominate any gathering, securing agreement to his own view and as quickly as possible, Donald facilitated a different kind of consensus, savouring the involvement.

Geoffrey and Donald both relied on their highly educated wives and they both had large families. But whereas Geoffrey actively controlled family life and plunged in wholeheartedly when he was at home and off-duty, Donald would come in, then stay in one place, recovering from his day. During my father's years as Editor of the *Economist* we were living in the house in West Hampstead. There was a flight of steps up to the front door and a flight of stairs up to the hall. In between there was a small area with a wooden chest and a cloakroom to one side. My father would lean on the chest for a few moments, looking at the post or any library books that had arrived, sticks hooked over one arm, before going on up into the sitting room, where he spent the rest of the evening. I could join him or not, as I liked. During the week, we might hardly speak to each other. Geoffrey's behaviour at home seems to have been exactly the same as it was at work. My father's was quite different.

When Geoffrey appointed Donald as Editor of the *Economist* in 1956, he described their relationship as one of 'interlocking temperaments and capacities. I am as sure as one can ever be in advance that it will work well.' Geoffrey himself became, successively, Managing Director, Deputy Chairman and Chairman of The Economist Newspaper Ltd. The editor was in theory, and legally, independent, but in creating the new role of managing director, Geoffrey remained the boss and was often in the office. Gordon Lee, *Economist* colleague and Donald's friend, commented on the set-up:

Donald was an extremely competent professional who had the ability Geoffrey himself lacked, of being both companionable and a shrewd judge of people. Geoffrey knew how useful this was. He knew what Donald had done in the past and he saw what Donald could do. There was genuine loyalty. Geoffrey could also say to himself: 'I've made you, you're mine'. Further differences between the two men soon emerged, however, straining the 'interlocking' harmony.

Donald was a moderniser. As well as a commitment to news reporting, after his years on *The Times*, Donald literally reshaped the *Economist* in terms of layout, typeface, colour and design, aspects of the paper that did not much interest Geoffrey. The *Economist* was known as a journal of opinion but Donald was incapable of not seeing it also as a newspaper. And unlike Geoffrey, Donald could be hesitant in his writing. He might insert references to immediate events into an existing article rather than accept that the article needed to be re-written. As if he was expecting a challenge from someone in authority, to whom he would be able to say, 'Oh, but I did mention that, didn't you notice, in the fourth line of the third paragraph.' Geoffrey was always in a hurry, Donald always cautious, a tension that would eventually break.

In 1956 Donald not only found himself in an ambiguous position professionally, he also came into a workspace that was on the brink of spectacular change. During his years as Assistant Editor in pre-war Bouverie Street and then by Waterloo Bridge after the Blitz, the paper was produced by small teams of writers in small rooms. Working life was a continuous academic seminar for which experience of Fleet Street journalism was irrelevant. Articles resembled essays written by clever undergraduates with strong opinions and no word limit. It was the compositors who shaped the hard copy, arranging and typesetting for the printers. Under Geoffrey Crowther's editorship the paper's reputation and scope grew significantly after the war and he became keen to move from the modest office at 22, Ryder Street, where the paper had been since 1947, ambitious for a suitably impressive landmark building. A group of three buildings on St James's, complete with Tower and Plaza, was officially opened in 1964. The preceding years of legal and land ownership negotiations, along with decanting to a temporary office in Conduit Street and then moving into the new offices, added major practical disruptions to the difficulties of Donald's editorship.

I remember that smart new space. Designed by Alison and Peter Smithson, it was the setting for my father's final years on the

Economist. During the school holidays my father would give us a ride into town. I knew little, then, about his demanding routines or the increasing strains of his fragile tenure but he was nevertheless happy to bring us into the place where all this was going on. We might be going shopping or we might just be passing the time of a free day. He was still proud to be there and he was indifferent to the boundary between private and public life as he introduced us to his colleagues. The exteriors are simple: fossil-inscribed Portland stone and glass. Reception and public meeting rooms on the top floor were lavish, however. I can still see walls covered in green or mauve silk. My own last visit to these rooms was for the reception following my father's memorial service in the autumn of 1981. The editorial department was one floor down.

There was an office car to take my father to work, a Humber with squeaky seats. My father would sit in front beside the driver, chain smoking. We sat in the back and squashed up when they halted in Abbey Road to collect Marjorie Deane, the *Economist*'s financial editor. She had to put up with Dad's smoke and ash floating back in through the open window. My father never learned to drive. The technology to adapt cars for a disabled driver wasn't available in the 1920s and 1930s and after the war it was too late. He was by then working on a daily paper and commuting into town from Essex. He would never have driven there and back every day. Wally was his driver throughout the roller-coaster years of 1956–65. There was a confidence between them, a friendship and loyalty. In August, when the rest of us were already there, Wally would drive my father down to Walberswick and go on up to Kessingland near Lowestoft, where he had a caravan.

The *Economist* comes out on Friday. Wednesday is deadline

day. Thursday is press day. On Tuesdays, Donald had lunch. This was his long-standing tradition. It was hard for him to go out and meet people, so they had to come to him. He was a member of the Reform Club but dragging himself up the great flight of stairs to the front door became too exhausting. As well as Cabinet ministers, diplomats and international visitors, there might be a copy editor, a sub-editor, even a secretary round the table, quite different from the days of Geoffrey Crowther. As a person Donald was not a snob. But as Editor he did like to mix with the great. Not for personal vanity. It was institutional vanity. He didn't want to be Editor in order to mix with the great. He wanted to be Editor in order to do a good job on the paper, which he came to personify.

On Wednesdays there was writing and editing. With the writing of his colleagues Donald trusted his instincts, saying yes or no fairly quickly. With his own writing it was different. After drafting a piece in neat and spiky handwriting, he would add corrections all over the place, compulsively qualifying his arguments in green ink. This was a habit Donald brought with him from *The Times,* where you had to be so careful because what you were doing was so much more important than you yourself. As a colleague said:

> However ponderous or pompous he was, what you got when you met Donald and got to know him was a decency and honesty and a humility which Crowther didn't have. He always wondered, Donald, in his heart of hearts I suspect, how he got there…

Wednesday evenings could be tense. Donald had to get the paper together and over to the printers before the messenger's last round. There was always a hold-up. Nothing to do but be anxious. And talk. And drink. And maybe confess your frustrations, as the myth of editorial independence increasingly came to light.

One evening in 1963 Geoffrey Crowther took Foreign Editor, John Midgley, out to dinner at the Dorchester, where he was a director. He announced that he wanted a younger man as Editor. Midgley advised him that potential candidates were stuck in junior positions, so if he really did want a young replacement for Donald he would have to create the chance for someone to be promoted. Geoffrey did take some of the junior members of staff out to dinner but Midgley comments that 'he didn't really have much of a touch with the young'. Geoffrey wanted to achieve the change quickly. It took two years.

Donald loved being Editor. He loved the media attention and the international contacts. He loved the lunches. But he had a poor head for drink. This became general knowledge after an appearance on BBC television's *The Brains Trust* in 1962 when he had drunk too much in the green room. 'You never saw him except a hand come out for a glass,' said *Economist* colleague Reggie Forty. *Private Eye* ran a cartoon under the heading 'Econopissed'. The next day Donald offered to resign but this was rejected. I remember my father falling out of the taxi onto the pavement outside our house after the TV programme, a dreadful irruption into our ignorance of his professional life. We stood about in the front garden in the dark. I don't remember him allowing any of us to help. Perhaps he went up to the front door on hands and knees.

In those early days of television the exposure would have been dramatic. If the story had been confined to the papers the attention would have been far less. Fleet Street journalists were incredibly hard drinking. My father only needed a couple of glasses to get tipsy and he never had a hangover, so there was no disincentive. And it was doubly visible, for Donald looked as if he was about to fall over anyway. My brother Christopher has a corrective view. He told me that because of his instability, my father had been taught how to fall. This meant going with the momentum of falling rather than trying to resist it. To minimise the impact of a fall, Donald made it appear more serious than it was.

My mother kept out of it. She said her aim had always been to let Donald be as independent as possible. Like his own mother. A colleague and friend once asked my mother if she could get him to cut down on the drinking:

> She gave me quite a moving speech, saying that if you'd seen the effort he has to make with his disability and the privations and discomforts and humiliations he has to endure – if you knew the scale of his exertions, you would not be nagging at him about whether he should drink or not, you would leave him alone. Well, she may have been only 85% right and not a 100% right, but she was more right than wrong.

When I discovered this years later, I was amazed. As far as I was concerned, her way of coping was to pretend it never happened, that it was in fact worse for her than for him. I could not imagine her saying to him, 'Yes, that was a disaster, but don't worry about it, it's one night's telly, they always put too much booze down your throat anyway, you are still you, get on with it.'

By now Donald was no longer the man Geoffrey had trusted to edit the paper. Wanting to get rid of him, however, had more to do with politics than personalities. This came to a head over Cuba in 1962. Stung by US criticisms of an equivocating *Economist* leader on the crisis, Geoffrey became defensive and looked for someone to blame, even though he had been actively involved in last-minute revisions. He was impatient. He could have tried to get rid of John Midgley, main author of the offending article, but Geoffrey focused on Donald because this already suited him. He wanted the paper to be more explicitly pro-American. He didn't want Donald to think he could 'turn the *Economist* into a leftist magazine'.

Geoffrey never forgave Donald for Cuba. He was immovably committed to American foreign policy and the country's status as an emerging post-war World Power. He also had a deep emotional commitment to the States. It was the country of his personal awakening, when he visited on a year's scholarship straight after university. It was his wife's home. Geoffrey was always clear that his allegiance to America was unswerving, that his politics were of the 'extreme centre'. Donald was more equivocal.

Donald was General Secretary of the International Press Institute in 1961 and chaired the annual conference in Tel Aviv that year. Geoffrey did not appreciate that, for Donald, getting together with international editors had nothing to do with left-wing or right-wing.

Donald would be very happy to get the editors of the New York Times, Washington Post, Izvestia, Pravda and the Frankfurter Allgemeine-Zeitung, Le Monde and so forth all together. The only people of this lot who would not seem like dangerous leftists to Geoffrey Crowther were, I suppose, the editors of the Washington Post and New York Times. Donald was the editor of the Economist and he was very glad to be seen on top of a bus, or anywhere else, conferring with the editor of Le Monde and the editor of the Frankfurter Allegemeine-Zeitung... Donald did quite a lot to keep detente alive in the press world. He liked to see the press as an international form of life. (John Midgely, *Economist* colleague)

For my father, it wasn't just that he was sociable or that the glory of his high office was satisfying in itself. It was much more than that. As my mother said, talking was movement for him. Literally. Conversation was his mobility. Something of this may be shared by all journalists but for Donald sitting down and talking with others was to become their equal in every way, disability out of sight.

Donald Tyerman, 1964

Geoffrey Crowther wanted to get rid of Donald quickly but the process was drawn out, obscure and cruel. From the start of his editorship in 1956, when he was nearly forty-eight, my father had only a two-year contract. Donald did not expect his term to be a long one but he was, at least at first, expecting to stay till he was sixty. Donald described himself as 'a servant of the paper'. In a note ahead of his resignation in 1965, he wrote to Geoffrey: 'Always, since you called me back to take your place, I have…left the determination of events, and my practical and financial place in them, entirely to your friendly disposition, and have no regrets for it.'

It's upsetting to hear the acquiescent tone though I know it was in character. I now understand how far it was exacerbated by sustained pressure and at a time when he still had the task of editing the paper. Moreover, what happened with Geoffrey at the *Economist* was a variation on what had happened with the Board of Directors at *The Times*, a long, uncertain period of responsibility without power. Donald edited the papers and put them to bed day after day, week after week, month after month, year after year. How this must have drip-fed his frustration and his physical decline. I can see him sweating across the short distance from his desk to the conference room, heaving himself stick by stick as the cherished role of Editor was peeled away and he was left isolated. Daily routines filled up with anger and pain, against the contrary pull of his dogged devotion to the job.

My father's admiration for Geoffrey Crowther never faded. Again, my mother stood back:

Geoffrey was so clever and yet he never made any effort to charm people. I mean if you've got total self-confidence. He could dazzle people with his brilliance and they all realised they were lesser mortals. He made it very clear that they were. I used to say, 'He could write in three short sentences making absolutely clear some obscure point which would take anybody else two pages'. This was a gift, it wasn't anything he did, he just had that gift. He was quite cruel to people, though, I think. I don't know how he and Don got on so well, they were very different. Don posed no threat to him, ever. Geoffrey was jolly lucky to have someone like Don quite honestly. Don was not in the least bit grand. He was pretty ungrand.

I now wonder if she stood back at home too. Despite her deep-rooted support for my father, perhaps she, too, was losing her nerve and gave my father a silent message not to bring any of it home. So they both had to cope alone with overwhelming stress, generating a potentially volcanic and mystifying calm in the spaces of my adolescence. I understand the anxious retreat from intractable problems. There was no way to throw things into reverse. But I wish they had tried to fight through, at least as far as a shared black humour. I wish my mother could have tolerated the noise.

Geoffrey Crowther left the *Economist* when he had surpassed inaugural editor Walter Bagehot's record of seventeen years. He wanted recognition on a broader stage. The next step would be fatal. He finally met an opponent who, initially as dazzled by him as my father, stared him down. The hotel chain Trust Houses had a long tradition of including an economist on its board and through his connections to the Cadburys, Quakers like his American wife, Crowther had been a board member since 1943. Trust Houses was not a purely profit-making company. It was more like the John Lewis Partnership.

A merger between Trust Houses and the hotel and catering chain Forte Holdings Ltd was mooted by Charles Forte in 1970 and reached through secret negotiations. The companies were complementary, the deal auspicious. It was agreed that Crowther would be Chairman for the first year, succeeded by Forte. Forte acknowledged Crowther's 'brilliant mind and impressive achievements' and he himself longed for status: 'You must be able to write your signature as if you were Nathan Rothschild'. But he found Crowther's assumption of control provocative, later going so far as to describe him as a 'swindler'. Both men were attracted to informality in business dealings, implicit arrangements that could be refuted later.

Crowther operated with minimal discussion and set office hours. Forte said, '…you could be trampled in the rush at 5.30' outside the Trust Houses office. Forte was the upwardly mobile immigrant's son, with 'knowledge, experience and love' of his company, who managed by 'common sense'. For him there was lots of talk and no fixed working hours. He was immersed in family and business and there was no separation. Crowther showed little interest in the daily life of the company he enjoyed running and his exceptional talent for clarification was of limited use in the world of business. Geoffrey's sister-in-law, Anne, spoke of Geoffrey's naïve integrity:

> When you're coming up against a person like Forte, you've got to realise that his judgment is different, and Geoffrey was really so full of integrity that he wouldn't believe the ruthlessness of a person who could be head of a business such as Forte wanted to be, how he could do it without shame. I suppose he cannot have re-alised how somebody like Forte gets to the position he is in. Forte had to fight for everything and Geoffrey stepped in at the top.

The long struggle for control between Crowther and Forte came to a head during the winter of 1971–2. Charles Forte threw all his energies and financial muscle into resisting Crowther's unilateral tactics. Donald never stood up to him. Like my father, Charles Forte had been charmed by Crowther. Unlike with my father, it soon wore off. After all, Forte owned Forte Holdings. My father owned nothing, not even a share in the *Economist*. In the showdown with Forte, Crowther was forced to confront conflict head on, and out in the open. He lost the protracted boardroom battle and his resignation became inevitable. He died within a month.

Of the three men, born within a year of each other in 1907–8, Charles Forte was the only one to write his memoirs, when he was eighty. Geoffrey Crowther died at sixty-five, my father at seventy-three. Charles Forte died at ninety-nine. Forte's ghosted autobiography has a righteous tone and a battlefield rhetoric. Crowther's sudden death is not mentioned.

Geoffrey, second-generation educated and going from public school to Cambridge, was a dominant insider in all but one of the worlds of his adult life. Donald, first-generation educated, going from a municipal secondary school to Oxford, never really belonged. He retained a sense of luck and amazement at his progress. You could not describe them as friends. They did not talk freely, as Donald did with other *Economist* colleagues. Donald was a sub-plot in the excitements of Geoffrey's public life. A constant and necessary figure but of late an annoyance.

The PHS lift waits as the two men take stock of each other. 'Donald,' says Geoffrey. 'My dear chap,' says Donald. They are each at the height of their career. The lift carries them on down.

As We Move

Unearthing the story of my father's relationship with Geoffrey Crowther was dispiriting. I felt myself descending with the two obituarists as the lift in Printing House Square returned them to Queen Victoria Street by Blackfriars Bridge. Then I made a discovery that shed quite another light on the events of the early 1960s. I learned, again, how different are the inside and outside of relationships and how many are the ways we make sense of them.

The story of a tree is held in its rings, whose breadth is as essential as deepening roots and the upward stretch of trunk. I have begun to think of family stories in the same way, stories that go round and round, this circuitry as vital as any chronological up and down. I found a set of papers – all new to me – that together told a story about my father at the time of his resignation as Editor of the *Economist*. As I turned back each layer to get to the core, I found that the story folded back on itself and that the end connected to the beginning. The story went round and round and takes its place in the family tree.

First, there's a strip of newsprint, pink with age. No date, no name, just 'News' and 'Page 3' in the top right corner and 'TV' underneath in bold. The article is a review of a programme from the night before written by Monica Furlong. 'Watching Mr. Donald Tyerman being interviewed last night in BBC2's *Encounter* series,' she said, 'I was struck by how few others on television achieve his effect of effortless charm.' Unalloyed praise for my father at a time when, I now know, things had not been going well for him for some years. I emailed Louise North, archivist at the BBC Written Archives in Caversham Park near Reading, to ask if there was any record of the programme. Even though I did not have the date she quickly replied to say that she'd found a transcript and would send it on. I looked forward to the evidence of his 'effortless charm'.

The programme was broadcast on 29 April 1965. My father had just resigned the editorship of the *Economist*. Monica Furlong was a well-known biographer, a Christian commentator and a regular contributor to the *Daily Mail*. Now I had the date and the source of her review. Donald was fifty-seven. His professional career was in decline, there were money worries and he longed to get away from London. Perhaps he was already feeling the rumblings of the emphysema that would nearly destroy him six years later. Furlong saw something different:

> Intelligent, relaxed, seemingly without facade or aggression, despising the kind of jokes and anecdotes which are the usual devices for avoiding penetrating conversation, he talked absorbingly about politics and economics, about the Press in

general and the *Economist* in particular. Listening to Mr. Tyerman last night I got the feeling for the first time for months that there really might be some way through the thicket of political and economic thorns, in the midst of which our nation sleeps on. I wish they could have him on again and discover which elements in our society are likely to play the trauma-healing Prince.

BBC TV current affairs moved down from Alexandra Palace in Muswell Hill to Lime Grove in Shepherd's Bush in the early 1950s. Studio G was vast, long and narrow, with a production gallery above the main entrance. My father would have had a stifling, protracted and disorienting trek through the dim warren of corridors, stairways and fire-escape ladders surrounding the former film stages. When he reached the set, a plain table and three chairs tucked into a corner of the huge space more often used for light entertainment – *Hancock's Half Hour, Blue Peter, Juke Box Jury, Steptoe & Son* – he was surrounded by a dense black forest of lights and cameras, each one fixed in position by block and tackle. It was hot and dirty, with sound-proofing like old sacks, a tap dripping somewhere and a phone flashing in eternal hope of an answer. As I read the transcript I kept in mind the creaky mechanics of black-and-white transmission in the old film studio.

My father was invited onto the *Encounter* programme because of his valedictory article in the *Economist*, which he had entitled 'As We Move'. Kenneth Harris, writer and journalist renowned for in-depth interviewing, chaired the discussion. He began by asking Donald to explain the title. Donald said it was from Tennyson, chosen for its theme of change: for himself, for the economy and for the country. Harris thought the tone of the article was pessimistic and asked

Donald what he meant by a British indifference. Not the idleness that the British were often accused of, Donald answered, but indifference to the technological and other economic opportunities that people in other countries found exciting. He described the British as 'unalive'.

Philosopher Bernard Williams was the third participant. He argued that as Donald hadn't explained any of this in his article we might assume he meant 'pull your socks up'. At this point in my reading of the tatty typescript, I sniffed a donnish tone rising off the page and I wondered how it would have come across on television. Professor Williams, wavy-haired and telegenic, Donald, ruddy and balding. He prefaced his reply to Williams with an apparent concession, 'It's obvious that one should be quizzed in this way', but went on to define the task of a valediction. It's an end, he said, carefully didactic for the philosopher, not a beginning, and he hoped his conclusion was clear from the article.

Donald was also pessimistic about the atomic bomb. He thought its use likely and that the 'problem underlying the bomb – the haves and the have-nots', would not be solved in present economic conditions. But he was optimistic about domestic affairs.

> We were exhausted after the War, perhaps more than any other country. Nevertheless, during my thirty years as a journalist we have accomplished triumphantly a political and social revolution. But we have not achieved the technological and educational revolution necessary to see what our new role in the world will be and to be excited about it.

Williams asked for more detail about this educational revolution. Donald said he was a great believer in the Robbins Report of

1963, which advocated the expansion of Higher Education, and he passed a critical eye over all three of them in the studio:

> We have the best education in the world for the cultivation of a particular kind of elite, I mean for the man who wins his scholarship in the sixth form and the man who gets his First in his three years at university – this is absolutely splendid. But I don't think it produces the kind of people who are, in fact, going to be excited or particularly latched onto the opportunities and needs and requirements of society of the present time. We find it extraordinarily difficult to overcome the belief that certain kinds of people are the right kind of people to administer this country and run its politics. We still believe, to some extent, that trade and business and industry, these things are not really as reputable as being a professor of philosophy, a civil servant, or indeed as being an editor of the *Economist*.

Harris asked about the international scene. What was Britain's role in the world today, post-empire? Donald said Britain's role was 'just to live and earn its living', to balance its accounts in the economic, financial sense. Our 'future,' he said, 'lies in the closest possible dovetailing with Europe' and with the maintenance of 'its relations with the wider Atlantic world'. Williams asked about the 'strain' between being pro-Europe and pro-America? If de Gaulle goes, will things change and Britain be allowed to sign the treaty of Rome? The *Economist* was notably pro-US. Donald said he saw no necessary conflict between the Atlantic alliance and closer relations with Europe and he raised the argument, used by both Tory and Labour politicians, that going into Europe meant surrendering national identity:

The extraordinary thing is that if you go into Germany, nobody ever says this at all. They're terribly European and they have a great sense of German identity. They don't believe that membership of Europe is a surrendering of their identity. There are a great many Frenchmen who have the same view.

'Well, I must say,' exclaimed Bernard Williams. 'With all credit to the *Economist* under your leadership, surely it was the *Economist* who recommended that we ought to move the administrative capital of Britain to the middle of Europe.' I see the professor leaning back from the microphone with a smirk after his bulls-eye. Donald said: 'I thought this was a splendid idea.'

Williams was sceptical about the *Economist*'s tradition of anonymity, magisterial and impersonal. 'We don't know who we're dealing with,' he said. Donald responded with his customary bow: 'I think that is always a danger that they [leader articles] become pontifical', and he quoted Lord Bracken, of the *Financial Times* but also publisher of the *Economist*, who said that 'there is only one three-decker pulpit left in London and that is the *Economist*'. However, Donald continued:

> Argument goes on inside. The editor of the paper may have the last word but in between the whole discussion goes on, and if one can't make up one's mind, one thinks aloud in the paper itself. But one is never handing down tablets of stone... The *Economist* and *The Times*, are made with hands, I mean, like the BBC.

As editor Donald was frequently criticised for being too even-handed, not fond enough of stone tablets.

Lastly, Harris asked Donald what he was going to do in his spare time. 'Will I have more spare time?' Donald replied. 'What will I do with it? I wish I knew.'

I'm excited and rather frightened by this extraordinary change… If you're a journalist, as you know from your experience, you have a treadmill and you have a deadline, and you have an alibi for everything, you never have to determine how you are going to use your time, you neglect your wife, you neglect your children, you neglect your friends and you always have an excuse because your time…is determined by the treadmill and the deadline, and all of a sudden the treadmill goes, the deadline is gone and you have to make up your mind for the first time what you're going to do at a given time, where you're going to be, you no longer have an excuse when you don't want to do this and want to do that and you can actually see your wife and children and friends again and this is a tremendous moral challenge.

Donald's conclusion reads like Cicero in open court or a Shakespearean recessional on stage, subordinate clauses rolling off his sonorous tongue. I can see why he made such an impression on Monica Furlong. In her review she didn't mention Bernard Williams once. This was live, unscripted TV, but Donald's fluency looks primed, the culture of his youth flowing directly into his words. I wondered if he was looking at Harris or at Williams as he spoke. Or at us. Could he be sure his family weren't watching – seeing and hearing him say that it was going to be a 'moral challenge' to spend more time with his wife and children?

I cheer the prescience of my father's views on post-war British society, education and international relations. And I savour his trouncing of Bernard Williams' patronage. But I can see that his verbosity and resistance to toff-macho games would have grated. Yet his feints were subtle and clever, the sly educator taking people along with him towards agreement before landing a punch of opposition. Unlike the voice I can actually hear on the tape of the 1940 BBC Home Service interview with Keynes, this transcribed voice of 1965 is one I recognise. I never knew the young man of the war years but I was a teenager in the sixties and familiar with my father's mental and verbal tricks.

Donald's farewell article in the *Economist* was impossible to photocopy in the British Library. Lines would fall off the plate-glass whichever way I turned the volume, two months' worth of *Economists* heavily bound together. Just over two double-columned pages are entitled 'As We Move'. The cover of the issue for 17–23 April 1965 shows Ian Smith. Rhodesia was the main story. After nine years as editor Donald wrote his first and last signed article. It was difficult. He couldn't say anything new without being accused either of not saying it before or of undermining his successor. He couldn't 'pontificate, prognosticate or prophesy'. He could only 'muse'.

Donald became editor of the *Economist* at the time of the Suez crisis in 1956. During his tenure there was also Russia and the Cold War, Khrushchev, Macmillan, the 'cracking of the Common Market', nuclear China, the Western Alliance and de Gaulle's 'second coming'. There was Africa and the independence of former British colonies. There was Europe's 'economic miracle – and Britain like love locked out'. Another Victorian reference here to join his Tennyson quotation. Anna Lea Merritt's 1890 painting of cupid pushing in vain at the mausoleum's door is indeed an image of grief, though what lies behind the door is death itself not a 'miracle'.

There were the United Nations and the Commonwealth, 'twisted out of shape by the new nationalism'. There was Cuba 'which made John Kennedy's little reign lasting history. And all the time, from Anthony Eden's Suez to Mr Callaghan's balance-of-payments budget last week, the crux for Britain itself has been, having lost an empire, to find (and earn) a role in the world. Am I, I wonder,' he wrote, 'after these years of change, optimist or pessimist?'

Change was just another name for history, he said. The litmus test for politics was how change was regarded. The Labour left pressed for change everywhere and all the time. Others resist change all the time. Donald argued that 'the way of sense is a third one in both politics and business.' Change should be used 'in pursuit of both interest and principle, to strive all the time for the possible whose margin fades forever and forever as we move'. Donald does not refer directly to Tennyson in the article but here's the source of his title, the poem 'Ulysses'.

Donald was pessimistic because of 'the rarity of clear-eyed, discriminating and enthusiastically strenuous radicalism'. There was a 'gleam' (Tennyson again) of this when the Tories tried to become European and when Labour was aiming to be re-elected in 1964. But now? Britain was better off and happier than it was in the 1930s, Donald wrote, but 'indifference makes the average British performance so much lower than the best. It is imagination and adaptability and industriousness that run too shallow.'

After reading Furlong's review and the transcript of the television programme, I am expecting the oratory. Here it comes: '…there is not the thrill and pride, the hope, the zest and the satisfaction, as well as the effort, which are the start and finish of everything in any society'. I can imagine an editor wanting to cut most of this for being vague and repetitive. I've done some cutting too, to relieve the weight of Donald's words.

Donald concluded by admitting that his article was a 'compote of the *Economist*'s own clichés', but 'perhaps none the worse for that. It is what we call in St James's Street, continuity'. It has been satisfying to edit the paper, he said, but 'never quite as satisfactory week by harried week as one would aspire to.' This was the closest he got in the article to saying what his life as Editor had really been like. From the outside it might largely appear to have been a period of success and stimulation. From the inside, the continuous strain, especially for the last two or three years, had become intolerable.

Here was Donald's characteristic style: a robust vernacular plus literary allusions, rolling repetitions and some windy sermonising. His commitments were clear: to a liberal third way, to a state defined as community, to Europe in conjunction with the Atlantic alliance. He was prescient about shifts in domestic politics. The televised discussion revealed personal opinions more vigorously expressed than was possible in his written valediction. Published three months after the death of Winston Churchill, my father's article takes me back to the political world of my youth: the real tensions of Cuba, JFK and the bomb, Macmillan and Wilson. For Donald to be invited onto the BBC2 television programme not so long after the humiliation of 'Econopissed', his departure from the *Economist* must still have been seen as a significant event. The lengthy in-house machinations that led to my father's resignation were not widely known.

To understand that Donald felt like a Ulysses, at the end of his public life, with its rewards and its dangers, which he had 'enjoyed greatly' and in which he had 'suffered greatly' – this hurts. Tennyson's

'Ulysses' is an old man. Donald was not yet sixty. The poem is a valediction, yes, but it turns out to be as much about possibilities as endings:

> Yet all experience is an arch wherethro'
> Gleams that untravell'd world, whose margin fades
> For ever and for ever when I move.

Ulysses was a sailor roaming the world, moving from life to death, 'I cannot rest'. Although this image conveys the opposite of my father's constrained mobility, a literal voyaging he could never enjoy, they share the restlessness and the experience of being cut off.

In the poem Ulysses is speaking to us, beginning with how he feels at this significant moment. Then introducing us to his son. Then paying tribute to his mariners. I can hear my father reading the poem aloud, as it should be, though I think he would have found it hard to get to the end without his voice cracking and tears in his eyes. Even the sea is described in terms of its sound, its 'many voices' as 'sounding furrows'.

Donald recasts Tennyson for the title of his own valediction. 'When I move' becomes 'As We Move'. The shift to first person plural draws us along with him. Attraction to the 'gleam' of the unknown represents an onward attitude, towards the unreachable horizon and the sunset. Donald was not an old man but his dream of escaping from chronic frustration was as powerful as the pull of never-ending experience. Donald had been thinking of retirement since 1963, when he bought Holly Cottage. Though originally expecting to leave at sixty, in 1968, by 1965 he must have been longing for it.

Ulysses dreaded retirement, inactivity, 'rust'. He was a 'grey spirit yearning in desire/ To follow knowledge'. This was like Donald, whose childhood realisation was that his place in the community would be through 'books and curiosity', following his 'bent' through hard work. Life's pressures made him a 'grey spirit' before his time.

'There lies the port': the Harbour with its open arms. These powerful images remind me of the paintings of Caspar David Friedrich, which are full of this natural-world symbolism. I saw them when I was in Berlin in 2010 to retrace my parents' Olympic adventure of more than seventy years earlier. I think of Bunyan, too, of course, and his *Pilgrim's Progress*, though his 'harbour' is a City. Ulysses is on a final voyage, 'to sail beyond the sunset'. 'The long day wanes' but there's still time to do 'some work of noble note'. Service to a higher cause was the mark of Ulysses. Donald saw the work of editing the *Economist*, as he had of editing *The Times*, as more important than himself.

Donald's love for Tennyson's poem was personal but also indicative of his generation. He learned the poem at school and his memory was prodigious. Celebrations for the 150th anniversary of Tennyson's birth on 6 August 1959 included a week of special BBC radio programmes. Donald's memory was refreshed.

Yet Donald was also the opposite of Ulysses. He couldn't respond to his own restlessness except with cycles of frustration and explosion. He lacked the resolve of the able-bodied sea captain. But he did cast off. And he was tired. From the 'effortless charm' of Monica Furlong's review to the combative TV transcript, to the resonant *Economist* valediction, these public records reveal the anxieties of the not-old man within, the innermost ring of the story.

Celebrating Donald's editorship of the *Economist*, 1965

Family Life: the flat

My father feared the 'rust' of retirement. What 'work of noble note' would be available to him now? As well as professional inactivity, there was the 'moral challenge' of re-entry into family life and the sudden loss of income. There were debts. Two years after my father's departure from the *Economist,* the house in Parsifal Road was sold. The top floor office in St James's was exchanged for a top floor flat in West End Lane. We later learned that my father had promised my mother she would always be able to stay in the house. She viewed the prospect of moving with dread. She remembered the fraught move from Brighton to South London after her father died when she was a child. The moves to London from Southampton in 1937 and back to London from Essex in 1951 were further contractions of her life, with irreversible consequences for her: the end of her academic work, the end of her public life, the end of local politics and the discussions she shared with Donald. My mother rushed it. All we had by way of preparation in the months before the move, when the still hidden money worries and the drinking increasingly affected my father's retirement, was the sound of their late-night rows. My brothers' bedroom was next to theirs. Christopher can still see the crushed plaster and cracked blue paint on the wall where he struck out to get them to stop.

We had no real idea of why we had to move and we weren't asked to help in any way. Three of us were still teenagers, four of us still in full-time education. I asked Anne recently how she felt when she was sent away at fourteen to avoid the ugly sight and sound of us fighting if we remained at the same school. She said she didn't remember this thoughtless decision as particularly negative. The time she did feel booted out was ten years later when we were suddenly piled into a flat on West End Lane that was too small for us, even doubled up. She had left university and had yet to start her career. Now she had no home. Anne quickly moved out to begin a life of determined independence. I was not as disturbed by the move as my sisters, certainly not as disturbed as my mother. Even though I was in my first year at university, I did not feel I was at a turning point in my life. I sit and think about this now but it still feels true. I wasn't unnerved by the coincidence of moving house and starting university. These major transitions were offset by powerful continuities.

All five of us went to the same university to read the same subject. You could say, how amazing. You could say, how awful. It's certainly unusual. Five Oxford historians. People looking in from outside the family often assume that my parents were pushy, maybe even hard to please if we did not live up to what must have been explicit expectations, that they ran a relentless machine. My insider memories are different. When I was a student, there was always a sibling around. This was true for all of us except Anne, who had three years to herself before I was born. Three years at home alone. University was more of the same, then, the family still there. I did not feel I had made any sort of active choice. I just sat there doing my homework, with the usual uneven results, and then wrote the entrance exam essays. I didn't I feel any pressure from my parents, only the self-stoked nerves of getting enough revision done. Going to university was just what happened next. Not far away and still inside the family.

When I was about fifteen I asked Ma if I could go to the youth club in Dennington Park Road. She said no. That was it. I don't remember what her excuse was but I didn't argue with her. It was like the prohibition on riding a bike. Even though we lived on a hill, there was hardly any traffic in those days, and the freedom of movement would have transformed my teenage years. My mother forbade us to ride bikes in London because she couldn't stand the row that would erupt wherever she drew the line between 'you can' and 'you can't'. I didn't push against her. To fight through a conflict to an agreed resolution was unheard of. The message silently modelled by my mother was 'I can't cope if you do this'. And, of course, in all these domestic matters, she was effectively a single parent.

Dad never spoke of his hopes for us or set up competitive targets or conditions of acceptance and rejection. They never tooth-combed through any school report. They left responsibility for my progress to the teachers and to me. I was often in trouble for talking too much or rushing my work but these were familiar criticisms. More serious was my retreat from tasks requiring a right answer.

I was conscientious but the results could be dramatically different: humanities good, languages and maths fine till they became too complex for me to learn by heart, sciences definitely borderline. My chemistry teacher's lie was kind. In her final report she wrote: 'Patricia tries hard'. Did anyone in those days know how my mind worked?

My mother was anxious rather than dominating. Like Dad, she never said what she wanted us to do with our lives. She hovered, supportive and nervous. She would rather we went to bed than stayed up late working. This was the family culture we absorbed. My brother Robert shares my view:

I only had one father. I don't really know if he was a good father. He sent us to fairly old-fashioned schools and I cannot remember going to him for any kind of advice. I cannot remember going to anyone for personal advice, I suppose I must have done. I think on the whole he would be pleased not to be asked. Because of his job and when he was on *The Times* he was always home late, he would get out of a lot. But I think we all admired him in a way, we admired the things he had done. I think he was bound to be a little self-centred because disabled people are. There are plenty of people who are not disabled who are self-centred. I think he was a very tolerant person. In a way that is one of the virtues of selfishness. He wasn't trying to interfere with our lives the whole time. He was interested in us but would never interfere in our affairs. I think he was happy with what his children were doing. We have been very boring. Perhaps it was good that our parents never told us what to do – we ended up doing it.

For a while my father remained involved with organisations and institutions that were important to him and they gave him public appreciation after the slow torture of his departure from the *Economist*. He was a Governor of the new Sussex University, a Director of United City Merchants and a valued member of the both the International Press Institute and the Commonwealth Press Union. Not surprisingly, his work as Treasurer of the Save the Children Fund was particularly precious, though unpaid. But there was no Wally, his loyal driver, waiting downstairs in a comfortable and ever smoothly running office car. Now it was my mother and a low-slung yellow Cortina with an irremovable Playboy Club sticker in the rear window and the battery of a Heavy Goods Vehicle. There was uncontrollable worry if anything happened to the car. So unlike those early days when my mother drove him all over the South East in that boxy Morris 8, establishing herself as his sole driver, a sign of their love and collaboration, energy and confidence.

Logistics for outings were elaborate, my father boiling with embarrassment as well as impatient to be off. Would my mother be able to park near enough to the flat? Would the people from the butcher's over the road remember they'd agreed to help get his wheelchair first down the indoor stairs and then down the outside steps to the pavement? Would the engine start first time or would it be better to warm it up earlier and hope it would later start at once? My father crying 'Damn and blast!'

When my mother found the stress too much, Mary or I would drive. Once I took my father to a meeting on the Embankment. As we approached the door of the building there was a lip of some sort. My father sighed with frustration. We had to keep going and it had to be fine. I pushed the wheelchair with all my might over this lip, using my hand to smooth the path of one of the small front wheels. No fingers were broken, though my wedding ring was compressed into an oval. Another time I borrowed the car to visit my youngest brother in Oxford to deliver the champagne for his wedding reception. On the way back to London that evening, dense traffic jerked forward onto the ring-road roundabout at Headington and the car behind rammed into mine. A rear indicator light was cracked. I thought of emigrating. I couldn't imagine walking into the flat in West Hampstead and telling my parents about the broken light as if it was just a broken light.

A recent conversation with sister Mary was a revelation. I was reminding her how I had longed to play the violin, a wish that was granted when I began secondary school. Soon one of the strings broke. No one told me violin strings break. Just as with the broken indicator light on the car, I couldn't imagine telling my parents. Perhaps Mary is right. Maybe at the age of twelve I was already shaped by my parents' anxiety.

Despite the core function of the huge yellow car, it would be a mistake to see it as having anything to do with real movement. Nor, when it wouldn't start or plans for getting my father downstairs and out into the front seat failed, that the car itself was the central source of his frustration. Yes, my father got out of the flat, the single space of his premature retirement, and, while he still had the physical energy, sustained some social life. But this wasn't the kind of movement my father had been used to for so many years. Movement for my father meant conversation. This was the greatest loss, up on the domestic top floor. Occasional board meetings were no replacement for a journalist's working life.

Christmas balloons

My father was particularly good at receiving gifts. I remember one Christmas in the flat at Buckingham Mansions when he was given two copies of the same book, a new biography of Arthur Ransome, whose *Swallows and Amazons* he used to read aloud to us on Sunday evenings at Parsifal Road. 'Ah, yes' he exclaimed, making the duplication an increase in delights rather than an awkward waste. 'I look forward to reading them both.' We believed him. Or if there were several jumpers, on they all went. The shirt, silk neckerchief and smart cardigan carefully chosen after breakfast disappeared beneath however many garments emerged from Christmas wrappings.

My mother didn't care for social formalities. She wouldn't arrange people in particular places round a dining table. Except at Christmas. Then she wrote clear name-cards. Not for reasons of protocol nor for any age- or gender-related balancing. It was to separate the Left from the Right. Guests who, by blood or old friendship, belonged to the extended family, reduced the tensions between parents and children, but it was still risky to mix ideologies, especially by the time the flaming pudding was consumed at dusk.

One year, maybe my father was sweating under several presents or was getting bored by an aunt or tipsy. Maybe some of the decorations we had tied to pictures round the walls were coming loose. He took a passing balloon and rubbed it on the wool of his topmost gift. Soon, it floated up to the ceiling and hung delicately in the hot air of candles, wine and terrible cracker jokes. Gradually, the dozen or so people round the table were drawn in, casting electrified balloons up to join his. A respectable aunt leapt up giggling like a flapper. A sophisticated émigré from Poland rose to the holiday-camp challenge and laughed throatily at the pair of pendulous globes she now sported on her elegant suit. The Right and the Left abandoned their reactionary and revolutionary tendencies to rub themselves vigorously with pink, yellow, green, red, white and blue balloons before launching them upwards. We watched them jostle aloft like bats, or like the Goons, who we knew lived on the ceiling.

Slowly their static halos evaporated and they shifted uneasily. They didn't fall onto our heads, however, but drifted delicately over to the nearest wall and slid down till they rested, at last, on the tip of the skirting board. It could have been science. It could have been art. It was an improvised ballet that held us together in unforeseen festive spirit.

Emphysema

During the autumn of 1971 Dad developed an alarming cough. He refused to see the doctor. He had a terror of hospitals after his childhood experiences. Instead, he sent my mother out to post letters to his bank and his lawyer, settling his affairs. When she did finally dare to call our GP my father was too weak to go to the surgery. X-ray equipment was brought up to the flat, a farcical scene straight from playwright N.F. Simpson – the machines could quite easily have spoken our weight or sung a Handel chorus as they wheeled along to the bedroom. The diagnosis was not the lung cancer my father feared. It was emphysema, which shouldn't have been a surprise for a long-time chain-smoking journalist.

Despite the repeated draining of his lungs, fluid kept returning, so he did eventually have an operation. More immobile than usual, on the ward my father's digestive system completely seized up. He was overweight when he went into hospital. My mother said 'he had a northerner's fondness for good, solid food, he should have lived on lettuce'. My father was in University College Hospital for more than three months. These weeks were exceptionally stressful for my mother. She had to be totally at his disposal at all times. She had to sit with him every day, from lunchtime until the end of visiting hours, just be there.

During the prolonged agony of my father's time in hospital, Alex and I were married. Our wedding was planned before he was ill, so that Alex's mother, a teacher, could come over from Canada in the Easter holidays. That evening we visited Dad in UCH, dressed in our finery. We gave him an audio tape of the ceremony, which I don't think anyone has ever listened to. I kissed him. A rare gesture, awkward and unbidden. He was so ill. I was not exactly sober. But I was moved and I'm glad.

How many of us students went East in 1968, inspired by the Prague Spring. I went to Hungary. Alex to Russia. Two months after the tanks ground into Charles Square we met at a concert in Oxford. He was full of energy and curiosity, confident, diffident, scholarly, with blue-eyed grace, fingers nicotine-stained from early-morning roll-ups. He played the French horn. I played my bassoon. As well as our music, there was art and travel. I loved it all, the great attraction, the huge affirmation, unexpected and thrilling.

When we both came to London I lived in a bedsit near the Oval, Alex in Tufnell Park. We met in the evenings at the Museum Tavern after he emerged from the British Library, unromantically commuting to opposite ends of the Northern Line at closing time. In 1971 I joined him in his shared house, where our bedroom had been painted dark blue and orange by the previous lodger, an Irish ex-seminarian. The wallpapered ceiling, all golden hexagons with indigo centres, created a perpetual starry night.

When my father left hospital in the late spring of 1972, he was a changed man, bearing a great sack of pills to take every day, which was unheard of for him. Going round and round on a walking frame to regain his strength was pointless. After so long in hospital his once-impressive upper body muscles had atrophied. Till the late 1940s he'd been able to stand at social events, both sticks hooked onto one arm, the other resting on a solid surface. He first used a wheelchair on a visit to Norwich Cathedral in the late 60s but now, just a few years later, he used one all the time. I was used to his tremendous willpower and self-control, used to him being able to do whatever he decided to. I thought he'd be able get back to where he was before he was ill. I failed to see that the incredible achievement, this time, was survival.

Back up in the flat he spent two weeks sorting out the books he wanted to take down to Suffolk when he could, at last, escape. He had a set of the fifty-four volumes first published in 1952 by Encyclopaedia Britannica in the United States as Great Books of the Western World. Dad chose Gibbon's *The History of the Decline and Fall of the Roman Empire*, *The Complete Works of Shakespeare* and Blaise Pascal's *Pensées*. I think of that child in hospital in Middlesbrough with those huge volumes of the 1910–11 Encyclopaedia. If my father told me he'd read the whole lot or every one of the Great Books of the Western World, I'd believe him.

Grandad T

Aunty Spot's Home Movies of the 1950s show my father on Southwold beach playing delightedly with Anne, his first child, blonde and charming. Thirty years later Elizabeth, his first grandchild, was born, another blonde and charming little girl, the first child of my youngest brother, Christopher. Between 12 February 1980 and 15 March 1981, Donald wrote fourteen letters to her.

Elizabeth was born on 28 December 1978. Donald can't rush to see her because he's not mobile and he's not well. He's over seventy now. He dies a month after his last letter. He won't be there when she's learned to read. His hello is also a goodbye. He is loving and playful, wistful and witty, telling stories about Elizabeth's parents and the 'Battery of Aunts', who he assures her 'will be no less formidable – and no less well-intentioned' than Bertie Wooster's. As in his letters to me decades earlier, Donald underlines every capital and rings every full stop, his ineradicable journalist's tics.

He writes from the flat in West End Lane just after they meet, when Elizabeth is about seven weeks old. He's been told she looks like this or that person but now he's 'quite decided that you look, splendidly, like yourself'. He remembers being blonde and charming himself till he was about three, when his hair was cut after he caught polio. Elizabeth's the 'miniature edition of all that is best to see in the family'. He signs himself 'Don', the name by which he is known to his family in the North. He adds: 'Grandad to you'.

In March 1979 he writes from Holly Cottage in Suffolk. Elizabeth was premature. Donald speculates that they might have shared a birthday. His was 1 March. He tells the story of his mother: 'A hundred years ago, my mother did the opposite. She was supposed to be born in 1878 but was born on January 1st 1879 – New Year's Day, which made that day important in our family celebrations, long before New Year's Day became a public holiday in England.'

Donald imagines Elizabeth 'looking very pretty now with the colour in your bigger cheeks'. He adds, 'Don't hesitate to ring up any time.'

In April he tells her he's looking forward to her visit in June. 'Men called painters and decorators have been busy getting your suite of rooms ready'. In May he writes, 'It was good of you to spare the time to stay with us while we were in London.' He won't see her at her great-uncle's seventy-fifth birthday party but he will be there for her own christening in Oxford. 'Bless you'.

In July he begins 'My dear Elizabeth Margaret', including her middle name, my mother's, her grandmother's. He describes the christening as 'your own pageant'. He hopes she didn't mind the sun, which he loves. They both hate the 'horrid green flies'.

He writes to Elizabeth on her first birthday. He knows she won't remember it. 'Only Scottish fiction writers, like Compton Mackenzie, pretend that they remember their first birthday.' Donald knows all this means nothing to Elizabeth now but 'it is all part of the family procession that you will realise later and you have a cousin coming soon.

Donald's next letter was written on 25 February 1980. 'Auntie Patricia now has a baby girl for you to play with – when she gets much bigger than she is now (the baby, I mean, not Auntie Patricia).' Elizabeth goes to a playgroup in Oxford. 'Many, many years ago there was a playgroup at another Oxford College run by a don who studied sums and photographed little girls. He also told stories, and one of these about Alice who lived in the college will be read to you very soon, I'm sure.'

In March, he writes: 'I'm told that when your diary is less crowded, and the weather is warmer, you will be bringing your Mother to stay with us again. This time you will be able to walk on the green and the heath and the beach, without your sheepskin coat. I may even give you a ride on my tricycle.' Elizabeth was not to have her ride.

In the next letter, Donald apologises for not writing for a while. 'If I delay much longer you will be writing to me!' But 'what I expect first is a telephone call from you telling me, in <u>my</u> own words, how your mother and father are behaving.' She's been staying with them over the summer and he wants to go on talking to her. 'We could see you growing up every day, and you would have grown up still more if you hadn't tried so hard not to sleep at all.'

In March 1981 Donald apologises again for not writing since her brother Edward was born five months ago. He thought of writing to him but has decided not to. 'He's still a bit young. After all, you can tell him anything he needs to know.' She is coming to stay soon and he's delighted, 'really delighted – provided you still remember me and my wheelchair. I hope the sun starts to shine by then.' Her father, Christopher, has just been awarded his doctorate: 'the sort of doctor who, whatever he may look like and however he may behave, is very wise and learned about some things. Hurrah! Love/Grandad T'.

This was Donald's last letter. But he did get to see her again. Here's the photo of Donald and Elizabeth in the garden at Holly Cottage in April 1981. He's in his wheelchair on the path. She's following on behind pushing her dolls' pram. It's nearly his last day.

Grandad T and Elizabeth, April 1981

Finishing Lines

When I explored Berlin in 2010, I saw that the most powerful memorials, like Gleis 17, were underfoot. Laid in the pavement outside apartment blocks in today's Berlin, brass tiles commemorate Jews who were deported from their home to the concentration camps. Cycling into the Grunewald area of West Berlin, I came across a row of five, an entire family. The mother, Rosa, was born, like Donald, in 1908. 'Hier wohnte Rosa'. The tile lies outside her flat alongside one for her husband and one for each of their three children. They were all deported to Auschwitz on 3 February 1943. I dismounted to look more closely at this wiped-out family, now returned to their neighbourhood in the form of the '*Stolpersteine*' (stumbling stones).

A strip of light catches the left side of the tile. Only a centimetre deep and it's enough to interrupt the sun. The right side is already fading into shadow. The letters inscribed on the left are thus emphasised: ROSA DEPORTIERT ERMORDET. Rosa is the one I notice because she was born in 1908, a coincidence that connected me to her, through my father. A reminder that human lives take similar shapes on different sides of any boundary. Rosa was only thirty-five when she was murdered. My uncle Harry was only thirty-one when he was killed a few months later: 1908 and 1943, the span of Rosa's life and two years of particular resonance for my own, through the lives of my father and his brother: two births and two deaths. The tile is smooth, the inscription bold. The pavement is made of stone and mortar that will crumble long before the brass.

I was not with my father when he died on 24 April 1981. I hadn't seen him since Christmas and my mother's phone call was a shock. The phone was in the kitchen. I went to stand at the bay window of what was then my study in our Archway house. I cried. Perhaps I was trying to tell a friend what had happened and it was saying the words out loud, words that my mother hadn't been able to say. Ma said, 'He's gone.' I was surprised by my physical reaction, as intimate in its way as the kiss I had given my father in hospital on my wedding night and so unlike the family habit. My first bereavement. He was only seventy-three. Good going, though, I realised, for a man with his shaky background and personal struggles, his life-long health problems and his daily endurance of stress and frustration. His older brother Reg had died six months before, aged seventy-eight. My father was the last of three brothers and two sisters. A long decline in physical strength, depression and isolation, and a great fear of returning to the total dependence of his early years – all these contributed to the ending of his life. He had flu. He died at home in his sleep.

On 28 April, a phalanx of metropolitan journalists in black over-coats stepped down from the London train at Darsham station. I watched them process down Westleton village street from Holly Cottage to my father's funeral in St Peter's church. Tributes were full of admiration and fond memories. I and my brothers and sisters hardly recognised this picture of the man we knew latterly as can-tankerous and depressed.

My brother Christopher read Thomas More's *A Dialogue of Comfort against Tribulation*:

> It were a long work to peruse every comfort that a man may well take of tribulation. For as many comforts you wot well may a man take thereof as there be good commodities therein.... Now because that this world is, as I tell you, not our eternal dwelling, but our little while wandering, God would that we should in such wise use it as folk that were weary of it, and that we should in the vale of labour, toil, tears and misery, not look for rest and ease, game, pleasure, wealth and felicity.... Woe may you be that laugheth now, for you should wail and weep. But as you see, he setteth the weeping time before, for that is the time of this wretched world and the laughing time shall come in heaven. Now must we in this world sow that we may in the other world reap: and in this short sowing time of this weeping world must we water our seed with the showers of our tears, and then shall we have in heaven a merry laughing time for ever.

The woe and the weep and the wail, the we and the world and the little while wandering before we find our merry laughing time. In the vibrant vernacular of 1534, More brilliantly matches sound and meaning. He was writing in prison, just before his execution. Donald did not share More's faith but he admired the steadfastness. And he loved the language of it, ringing alliteration conveying the deepest feelings.

Donald was remembered by people from all times and places of his life. Obituaries appeared in the *Daily Telegraph*, the *Financial Times*, the *Sunday Telegraph*, the *Guardian*, the Suffolk *Leiston Observer*, the *Hampstead and Highgate Express* and *The Tower*, parish magazine of the Essex village my parents lived in for ten years from 1941. David Astor wrote in *The Observer*:

> For more than a year Donald Tyerman would write the editorials and decide the policy of two papers, the *Economist* and *The Observer*. He performed this feat with occasional air raid interruptions and having to move everywhere on crutches due to polio. Tyerman, broadly a Social Democrat, applied his Yorkshire good sense and cogent style to playing a formative role, probably as great as anyone's.... He was enormously goodhearted to the young, and his services to *The Observer* and its esoteric wartime staff, were of the highest. Himself a real-life paterfamilias of outstanding success, he became a father to those of all ages who were creating the beginning of the postwar *Observer*.

The *Times* obituary appeared on 25 April 1981 under the heading 'Rock of Gibraltar at Printing House Square'. I paid particular attention to this one because of my father's agonising years on the paper. I was curious to see if any of the words were those commissioned so long ago from Geoffrey Crowther that day they met in the lift at Printing House Square and nine years after his own death.

I found the tone, facts and assessment of my father stilted and inconsistent. We are told that Donald was a 'professional editor rather than a journalist' because he'd had no apprenticeship in a newsroom or as a reporter, or in 'the humbler walks of journalism'. This would have been true of nearly everyone on the *Economist* before the war so it reads to me as unnecessarily negative. Donald is described as a 'cripple'. This may have been a remnant of Geoffrey's work but looks far out of place in an article published in 1981.

There are passages giving the impression that the writer did not know Donald, for example implying that polio meant that my father did not receive 'much schooling' as a young boy. The obituarist assures us that this lack of schooling 'did not limit his intellectual development' nor 'what is more rare, did it twist a sunny, outgoing character'. I can't imagine Geoffrey describing Donald as 'sunny' and it doesn't sit with the 'somewhat deprived and possibly too earnestly striving young man' who got his scholarship to Oxford from Gateshead Municipal Secondary School. These passages resemble the *Dictionary of National Biography* (DNB) entry for Donald written by his *Economist* colleague Norman Macrae.

The obituary acknowledges that 'had Barrington-Ward lived longer, Tyerman might have grown to be his natural successor'. With his family background and academic experience, Donald would 'contribute new bearings in what was to be a largely uncharted sea'. This was never the view of senior *Times* personnel but perhaps it was Geoffrey's. Perhaps a sense of Donald having been undervalued did, after all, play some part in his choosing Donald as his successor at the *Economist* in1955/6. The obituary acknowledges Donald's guidance of younger generations of colleagues, though implies that he was able to do this because he was stuck in his office chair and therefore had the time.

Donald's work with the International Press Institute, the Commonwealth Press Union, the Save the Children Fund and with LSE and Sussex University is described by *The Times* obituarist as 'peripheral'. He was 'too tied to the practice of journalism'. Thus a compliment is paid and withdrawn and the last sentence contradicts the obituary's opening.

Condolences from the wide range of organisations in which my father continued to be active are of course public tributes but they reminded me once more that outside opinion did not align with the views of the Fleet Street insiders. Kenneth Morgan, Director of the Press Council, of which Donald was a member from 1963–8, wrote about a 1979 TV debate on press freedom in which they both participated: 'Like everyone who knew him, I admired tremendously his skill and professionalism as a journalist and his integrity and courage as a man.'

Friends and colleagues wrote to my mother. The *Economist*'s John Midgley had found it hard to prepare an obituary for Donald while he was alive, which was the custom. After he died, he told Margaret: 'it was an extra source of grief that Donald couldn't be on hand to sub the copy and watch the proceedings. I wept for him.'

Donald after receiving his CBE, late 1970s

Donald receiving his Commonwealth Press Union award
from Gavin Astor, late 1970s

Mary Goldring, former Business Editor, then Deputy Editor, wrote:

> He was the wisest and kindest of men and I'm only one of hundreds of journalists who learnt so much from his guidance – and only learnt years later the battles that he fought for us behind the scenes. Without Donald, my career at the *Economist* would have been a decidedly short one but never did he so much as drop a hint about the trouble I caused him with the Directors, except once, I remember, when he asked to be briefed before a particularly awkward meeting.

Many who wrote letters in 1981 paid special tribute to Margaret. Donald's *Times* colleague Iverach McDonald wrote: 'I have done nothing but think of you and of him… It is when we think of how close you and Donald were for so many years, in a true partnership – that we begin to measure your loss.' Close *Economist* friend Gordon Lee wrote: 'Donald, to me, has always been and will always remain in my mind as a newspaperman's newspaperman…a man who said yes rather than no, a man I loved… The hole in your heart must be enormous.'

The letters acknowledged not only my mother's support and understanding in relation to Donald's public life but also affirmed that their life together was a partnership. This was not so clear to us as we grew up, when each parent moved in separate spaces and played such different roles in each of our lives. Their intimate life was hidden and they were not demonstrative in front of us.

A Memorial Service was held for Donald on 6 October 1981

at St James's, Piccadilly. In his address, Lord Robbins spoke about my father's 'very considerable' behind-the-scenes influence at the *Economist* as well as his public courage, for example, in his opposition to the government's intervention in Suez so soon after becoming editor. Robbins also spoke about their joint experience of being Governors of the London School of Economics during the student unrest of the late 1960s:

> It greatly impressed me that, despite personal friendship, Donald refused to adopt an attitude until he himself had interviewed members of the contending parties and had made up his own mind... To have Donald's support after this in such circumstances was a massive reinforcement of one's morale.

Margaret was furious.

It's difficult to describe Don and his life. Because of polio a great many things taken for granted in a normal family are impossible. His achievements were tremendous. His family, his great interest in sport and his gregariousness were compensations. He had a small band of thoughtful and devoted friends who came fairly regularly to the flat to gossip. They will never know how grateful I am to them. At his memorial service in St James's, Piccadilly I felt very cynical. The church was packed and I said to myself, if all the great and good who had given up the morning to attend had, each one, once in the previous ten years, spent that amount of time visiting Don, what a difference it would have made.

Chariots of Fire

Chariots of Fire came out weeks after my father died. The film begins with a funeral, at St Clement Danes Church, a few hundred yards from Fleet Street. Athlete and journalist Harold Abrahams was some years older than Dad but was known to him through radio sports commentating and was, I feel sure, a hero for him, even though Abraham's reporting of the Berlin Olympic Games was acknowledged to be over-emotional and erratic. Donald would have admired him for his marriage to Sybil Gordon, star of the D'Oyly Carte Opera Company, whom Donald saw playing Zorah in Gilbert and Sullivan's *Ruddigore* at Oxford's New Theatre in June 1929, an end-of-final-exams treat. Dad had loved 'G&S' since his schooldays in Gateshead, where the operettas were performed on Speech Day. Thirty years later he took us to see *Iolanthe* and *Patience* at the Savoy Theatre in the Strand, where he whisperingly explained all the political and literary references. He would also have admired Abrahams' attitude to athletics. Abrahams, who faced continuous, if coded, anti-Semitism, was also disapproved of for hiring Sam Mussabini, a professional coach, before the 1924 Paris Olympic Games, because this revealed a lack of true amateur sporting spirit. I am sure Dad would have been on the side of the professionals. However much he believed in the love of sport for sport's sake, Dad was never a 'gentleman'.

Stratford 2012

The 2012 London Olympic marathon was a three-lap circuit of central London's landmarks between Buckingham Palace and Tower Bridge. The race did not finish at the Olympic Stadium. Athletes did not run along Mile End Road, past my birthplace, the Marie

Celeste Ward of the (now Royal) London Hospital, nor the statue of Gladstone outside St Mary's Church, Bow, at the very edge of the City. Here was no memorial to the classic bearer of good news, the traditional re-creation of the long-awaited arrival of Pheidippides, the lone runner, the climax of all modern Olympic Games. The official reason for the toffee-nosed avoidance of the East End was 'security'. Instead, here was a Heritage Tour, as far from the fact and spirit of the heroic original as it is possible to imagine. The 2012 race, cheered by crowds enjoying a sunny day out among London's most spectacular buildings, was truly festive. I was there. As an Olympic marathon it was meaningless.

After watching two of the three laps near the plastic mini-roundabout below Tower Hill, I cycled out to Stratford. I could just see my father propelling his chair along the route, as he had to the White City more than sixty years before. He would have loved that ride as much as he would have hated the rebranded marathon. As he pushes and pulls on the chair's levers, speeding up and grinding down in his determined way, I see in him that characteristic doubleness: the strong upper body, an arm raised in greeting, and his legs, source of so much pain and frustration, weightless in their splints.

The last two lines of Dad's beloved 'Ulysses' by Tennyson are now inscribed along a wall in the Stratford Olympic Village, as they were at the South Pole in 1912, the year of my mother's birth. What inspired my father, however, were not the lines about striving, competing and winning but those about the vision of the arch of experience. The recognition that as our understanding expands it always recedes beyond the horizon. It's a dream. A dream of physical and mental freedom.

The Olympiastadion in Berlin flourishes as the home of football club Hertha BSC. All that remains of the White City stadium in London is the Finishing Line, engraved in the courtyard of the BBC's new offices.

I was with my mother when she died thirteen years later. She'd been living for a while in a retirement home near Westleton. She would ring and say, 'Get me out of here.' Companionship without practical responsibilities did not lessen her claustrophobia or anxiety. When the elderly women gathered in their rooms or round the fire in the hall for sherry, they didn't gossip – they sniped, making barbed contact with each other through family boastings or canvassing agreement on that day's particular injustices. They couldn't embrace this chance of late sisterhood.

While she was still living at Holly Cottage my mother had various support systems. Either someone was with her day and night, or a carer came for twelve hours overnight and local friends would come at certain times during the day. None of these arrangements worked. There were still decisions and paperwork. She still had her chequebook. The carers and some of the visitors were not people she would have chosen, and she couldn't get on with them. She would ring the agency and complain. They nearly struck her off the register. We discovered that she was paying the women she liked but not those she didn't.

They called from the home on a Tuesday morning. If we came straight away she would know us. If we left it till Wednesday she might not. I drove across country from my Open University office in Milton Keynes. I didn't hurry. She was alive. Driving slowly would keep her alive. I stopped to fill up with petrol about five miles from the village. By mid-afternoon we were all there, Ma lying in her high hospital bed.

I had driven down to see her with my daughter Joanna the previous Sunday. I did hurry that day and was stopped by the Essex police for speeding. They looked at fourteen-year-old Joanna and let me off with a warning. My mother had had a stroke before Easter. We worried that the retirement home would send her on to a nursing home or hospital but they never once raised the issue. From then on we organised a rota to visit during the week and at weekends. Soon, she had two more strokes, developed a cold, then pneumonia.

Joanna and I had found her dressed and sitting up in her chair by the window. Her breathing was difficult because of her blocked nose. She knew us and was chatty, though it was an effort. What she said connected to us two specifically and it ranged over the whole of our

Margaret at 80

lives. However, if we responded to what she said, thinking this would keep the conversation going and therefore be stimulating for her, it seemed to break rather than strengthen her train of thought and she would start on something new. So we listened and commented here and there. It was impossible to know how all this felt for her. She wasn't in discomfort and she wasn't restless.

Now, on Tuesday, we said hello and sat or stood by her bed, holding her hands, trying to hear what she said. She responded to each of us. Her breathing was noisy and her nose was running. We camped round, knowing and not knowing what would happen next. We drove to Leiston to buy toothbrushes, knickers and groceries so we could stay at the cottage. That night she was restless, struggling with her arms. They gave her an injection. My younger sister went home to be with her husband. The rest of us had an extravagant supper at the village pub. We shared this single focus. That was all there was and it was totally absorbing. Anne and I found a couple of her nightdresses.

In the morning she was bent over in bed, breathing noisily. She responded to touch and sound but she didn't know who exactly we were. The staff warned us. They were right. We sat with her, quiet and tense. We read a bit, talked a bit, went out for a brief walk in the gardens, went to the pub for lunch, for some air. Each time we left and came back she was more slumped and shrunk, crouched over. We watched her and wiped her nose.

That evening, she was noticeably weaker. We settled down in her room. I was sitting on her bed, holding her hand. Her breathing stopped. Then it started again. When she stopped breathing it was as if she was asleep, relaxed, still herself. It was only when she started again that I was frightened. Several times her breathing faltered, started again. The night staff came and sat with us, holding her and listening. She stopped breathing and did not start again. We sat. Holding our own breath. One of the women stroked the side of my mother's head, making sure. She nodded at us and went away.

She returned to say the doctor was coming. We went downstairs and telephoned the rest of the family. When we went upstairs again it wasn't our mother any more. Her face was waxy. They gave us sweet tea and told us stories of her life in the home. My brother called the undertaker. He said he believed that a person's soul leaves their body at the moment of death.

We went back to the cottage around midnight. Next morning I dressed in some of my mother's clothes and put on the jade necklace I had brought her back from my first visit to China. It turned out she'd left me the car she'd sold some years earlier. I should like to collect all the bits of my mother from all the other lives she had flowed into and make her stand up for herself, want to know herself, risk being visible, be bold. I want to pay her this much attention, for her sake and for mine, but it is hard to sustain. I feel the intimacy of her dependence and my habitual reflex to disengage.

My mother received her own public tribute. *The Times* obituary described her as 'a woman of ability, charm and courage' but noted she was 'caustic about those she regarded as fair-weather friends' of my father's. His final years were 'very tough and emotionally draining' for her. She once said that, if she wrote her memoirs, she would call them '*Reluctant Martha*.'

I imagine speaking to her:

I hear your voice, Ma, your familiar roll call of our names – Anne-Tricia-Mary-Robert-Christopher-Pickle-Magic. Do you remember Aunty Spot's films of our summer holidays in Walberswick? Watching them now, I am struck by the deep blue skies, the ginger sand on the beach and the luminous gorse up on the common. I see a constant milling about, children running in and out of the water, pedalling round the village on motley bikes, clambering onto a pony in the pub forecourt. Occasionally we stopped and waved. You are there, tall and substantial, helping us off with our clothes to go swimming, on with our towels afterwards, driving us all over the place, your right elbow resting in the open window. Sometimes you glance at the camera with a grin.

You didn't live long enough to enjoy the reassurance of mobile phones and their caller-ID. I am tempted to laugh at the thought of you struggling to get the damn thing out of its case, unlock the impossibly micro keyboard and press Answer rather than Media Album, or Reply rather than Equaliser. How unfair of me. During the war you were an Officer in the Auxiliary Territorial Services, the one in uniform, a professional driver and instructor of new recruits. You described your vehicle as a 'laundry-van turned ambulance, with one useable gear'. Making machinery work was what you did.

Which is more than I can say for myself. My laptop hates me. The screen flashes with language filched from the divorce court as it cites 'security reasons' or 'degradation' for refusing to boot up with its former cheer. Returning from a modest trip to France, where the computer behaved impeccably, I find myself staring at a black hole overlaid with my enraged reflection. Of course it's your face looking at me from the blank screen. Your wary self-consciousness pulled into lines of worry. We share that down-turned mouth, the high forehead and the thinning hair. My voice could be yours, too, as I plead with my laptop for a response.

Fifty years after stripping jeeps and re-tuning high street vans, you went to stay with Aunty Jessie, ostensibly to recuperate from a couple of weeks in hospital. She could also draw on skills honed in wartime. When that power cut plunged East Sussex into darkness, Jessie lit candles, made a fire, heated a pan of water with two eggs in it and forked up slices of bread to the flames. She had tea, toast, boiled eggs, light, warmth, and water for washing up. But it wasn't as simple as that, was it? You were a child when your father died at the tail end of the flu epidemic. Jessie was a teenager. The sound of your mother and sister crying and fighting, competitive in their grief and their genteel anxiety about money – this noise stayed deep inside. You found a way to telephone us from Jessie's house, hissing into the mouthpiece: 'Get me out of here.'

You managed to send a few letters. Mine began 'Dear Christopher'.

The cottage

My parents died a long time ago but we kept the cottage in Westleton for another twenty years. I still love the landscape of field and forest, heath, marsh and sea, but it was time to sell. I swept out the garage. Ma hid Dad's three-wheeler right at the back, behind the bikes, the logs and a few garden tools, where it slowly disintegrated. Anne and Christopher made several journeys to the municipal dump a few miles away, where skips are spread out in a square, one for each kind of material. Christopher heaved Dad's splints up to the rim of the skip for metal, stretched out his arms and let go. The splints rang down into the bottom of the bin, empty that morning.

Sorting through my parents' library in the cottage I came across two books published just before their Olympic adventure in 1936: John Maynard Keynes's *The General Theory of Employment, Interest and Money* and T.S. Eliot's *Collected Poems 1909–1935*. I doubt my father would have taken Keynes to read on the journey but he might well have taken the poems. 'Burnt Norton', one of Eliot's *Four Quartets*, is an enquiry into the nature of Time, whose contradictions he expresses with the phrase: 'At the still point of the turning world'. I sat down and read the poem, imagining what might have been my father's response. And what did I find? That so much of the poem speaks to the very atmosphere I have been trying to capture in my description of family life. Here were also, perhaps, some truths about my father. I think he would have responded particularly to Eliot's evocation of stillness, immobility and frustration, to the way in which the poet distinguishes consciousness from memory and to what he says about the absence of fear and desire. My father did not share Eliot's conviction of divine ordering or the possibility of redemption but I feel that he might well have shared Eliot's experience of tension, perhaps even the despair. I can see the English rose garden stowed in his pocket on the way to Berlin. The door never opened is a fundamental image of my upbringing.

Sitting close to the electric heater in the cottage sitting room, I invigilated the removal of furniture and books, waiting for my chair to be taken out to the van. At the far end of the next room the wall was light, clean and clear, indifferent to past or future. By the floor in the corner the plaster had fallen away, exposing flaky brickwork. I looked out at the row of poplars by the pond. I looked at the space where the hall table stood for fifty years. It was hard but I realised there was sadness before, when the cottage was filled with my parents' belongings but not inhabited by them. There were more ghosts during those years than I felt hovering now. The cottage was bright and broken. It needed a new life. Before it decayed to nothing.

What I have learned as a result of selling the cottage is that I am the only one of 'the children' who does internet banking.

When my father died in the spring of 1981 it was a shock. I cried after my mother phoned. The professional and physical crises of his final decades shaped our family life more than his exceptional achievements as a scholar, teacher and journalist. My mother couldn't adjust to being on her own, despite the protracted difficulties of recent years. I didn't understand this and I was often impatient towards her, ignorant of my parents' true bond. I wished she could enjoy the freedom and the peace but I forgot her dread of abandonment. Ma told Christopher that the first night she spent alone in the cottage was the first night she had ever spent in a house by herself. She was sixty-nine. Now I am about the same age and I see that it's a time of transition. My daughters and I look after each other. Later, the pivot will swing over towards them. In 1981, a new mother and new lecturer, in my inattention I didn't give Ma the support she needed. She was dependent and isolated, the reverse of my life as it is now.

My father knew nothing of the events that led me to write about how his life has influenced mine. I think he would have been hands-off, as usual, though concerned for my welfare. He wouldn't have said 'fine, fine', as he did when I was a teenager. He would acknowledge the threats to my health, the end of my marriage, my new partnership and the challenges of my adventuring in China, in writing. His letters would be long and circumspect, in the tiny, legible handwriting that was just like his mother Catherine's. They wouldn't contain admonishment or direct advice. Or specific offers of help, for that matter. But they would contain grit, his particular 'books and curiosity' determination that enabled him to live in a social and professional world. It is possible that he would find my problems too draining for much comment, given that he, too, was so drained in the last years of his life.

Our letter-writing might at last be finished. Yet I can't help wishing that I did have a set of letters from these years. He'd be reviewing my life or reviewing his. He might even have reflected on parallels between us. Or he'd be texting me at midnight or emailing me at dawn, online thoughts-for-the-day with quotations from Edwardian poets or historical and political allusions, as nimbly hands-on as any able-bodied father.

Conversation with an Alien

Searching the drawers of Dad's desk in 1981 I found his bottles of Quink, blue, black and green, some unused stationery, fading newspapers kept for significant articles, pink manila folders of official correspondence. I was dismayed by how little stuff there was in this chunky desk he had made in Southampton to mark his first job and the first study of his own, only the general admin and scattered holiday postcards providing random colour. A sad summary, I thought, till I came across a stiff brown envelope franked by the BBC. Inside was the foolscap transcript of his 1959 *Woman's Hour* talk. The story of his childhood. His largely unknown childhood. The revelation was rich and moving. I sat at the desk and I heard his voice, heavy and warm, at ease with his unseen audience, as he sat at the studio microphone and spoke to strangers. This was his metier.

Dad spoke of his families, the original northern one and the new southern one. I was engrossed. But as I read I felt myself trying to get a word in edgeways. I was in this story, too. A double image clarified. I saw Dad sitting in his study overlooking the garden in West Hampstead. The desk is at right angles to the window. He's writing, his meticulous legible handwriting, head bent over his work with the total concentration we so often saw when we were playing in the garden, and I saw him up there working. There's a radio on a shelf behind him and his voice speaks the words he is composing on paper. The programme is *Woman's Hour*, which in those days broadcast at 2pm just after *Listen with Mother*.

At the same time, I see myself sitting at a mirror image of his desk listening to the same words coming out of the same radio, the transcript lying in front of me. I am nearly the same age as he is. I am absorbed, impressed, disturbed, exasperated. I interrupt. To stop him talking about how 'lucky' he was or how I've inherited the nemesis of his 'wild rages'. Try to get his attention, to have a conversation. Impossible. I think how much conversation in a large family is impossible in the same way, everyone talking at once. If only someone would listen. Let alone agree.

My double image is a play without dialogue. It could be a radio play, suited to that medium, Dad's favourite. Except that the sight of it is essential: Dad up there in his study and me at the same age, sitting at the same desk listening to the same words. Parallel monologues. True to the special stasis, atmosphere, provocations and unheeded exchanges of family life. You have to see it. I called my play 'Conversation with an Alien', after the insulting judgment of *Times* board members, though I was advised that 'Alien' would lead to classification as science fiction.

A Separated Twin

China

I landed in Shanghai on a Sunday afternoon. The airport then consisted of single-storey sheds way out in farmland to the south-west of the city. Though they looked like sheds anywhere and the rich green and gold of summer maize crops looked like summer crops anywhere, none of the people looked or sounded remotely familiar. I stood there saying to myself, 'I'm in China.' I felt at ease. I couldn't have known in advance how I would feel, a stranger out there on the tarmac. My years of visiting China added to my understanding of who I was, layers that existed but only revealed by the Far Eastern perspective.

It all started with the magazine *Spare Rib*. My husband had bought the December 1986 issue for an article on women photographers. I caught sight of an item in the 'News in Brief' section at the back. Under the image of a female factory worker, I read that new legislation in China was to bring millions of people with disabilities into education and employment for the first time. The small paragraph on the back page set off an explosion of excitement in my head. These were exactly the issues I was concerned with at the Open University. I was due some study leave. There was to be a conference in Beijing in June 1988. I applied to the British Council for funding and I enrolled at the Society for Chinese Understanding in Camden High Street, North London, for classes in Mandarin. I laughed with anticipation as I began to imagine the possibility of going to China.

At first I resisted the cries of 'taxi!', 'taxi!', just as I would have done years ago when pestered in Rome or Athens. Eventually I realised I would have to say yes or be marooned. I ran after the last remaining vehicle and crammed myself into the car. I showed the driver the strip of scarlet letters on the letterhead of the Shanghai Education Department and used my sparse Mandarin to ask him to leave a message for my absent host and then find me somewhere to stay. To make conversation I used up the rest of my vocabulary telling him I was a teacher and that I had two daughters.

The hotel was in an area of town undergoing a massive transformation and everyone else staying there was Chinese. Attentive staff poured boiling water into vacuum flasks enamelled in bright colours, decorated with floating clouds and long-billed cranes. There were stuffed sofas with labels in Russian and Nescafe jars with labels in Chinese. In the morning I ate cold pickled vegetables and warm congee with overseas-Chinese engineers here in the city to build roads, bridges, factories and blocks of flats. In this utterly different environment I was sharply defined, as somebody and as nobody. Here, in China, on my own, I was visible but nameless. I found myself willing to be fascinated and absorbed. I still didn't know when or how I would make contact with my Chinese colleagues (I later found out my last letter hadn't arrived) but I was curious and light-hearted.

Then I spent five days in Shanghai with my host Yin Chun Ming, twelve years older than me, who spoke Russian from studying educational psychology in Moscow, and our translator Ye Lin, twelve years younger than me, a school teacher who had taught himself English without going anywhere. We were all born in the Year of the Pig. We ate ice cream in the park and we rode together on the buses. They couldn't afford to give me more substantial treats.

From Shanghai I travelled down to Hong Kong to join a pre-conference tour group. Staying in the new Sheraton Hotel near the Kowloon waterfront, I was captivated by the Island skyline at night and by crowded streets and pencil-thin high-rises during the day. My whole body was warmed by the moist tropical heat. I.M. Pei's angular Bank of China would be opened in two months' time, on the most auspicious day of all days: 8.8.88.

My second visit to Hong Kong was for a month's fellowship at Hong Kong University. The landing at Kai Tak airport was spectacular, the plane slicing down between blocks of flats, trailing noise and thick shadow like a giant beast, then racing towards the water at the end of a short runway. Shunting through the traffic chaos in Kowloon was nothing new for me, a Londoner, but the bucking ride up Conduit Road on the Island continued the airport fantasy. Tipping over into University Drive from Kotewall Road, I had my first sight of Robert Black College, built in the 1960s as a series of traditional Chinese courtyards, the university's residence for overseas visitors, named after this former Vice Chancellor and Hong Kong Governor. The sweep of the harbour was, in 1990, unbroken by off-the-peg science towers or up-market residential cylinders. There was no Tsing Ma Bridge hanging by a tarmac thread in the distance. The colour was intense: the green of the hillside, the blue of the college roof tiles. And, after the gear-grinding trip across town, it was quiet. The sudden peacefulness of the college, with its direct access up to the Peak, remained a treasured open secret.

The best route back down from the college to Central was the number 13 bus. I grew up on a number 13 bus, riding along Finchley Road every day to school at Swiss Cottage. In 1990, Hong Kong's number 13 was a cream and blue juddering double-decker, all windows wide open for a snatch of breeze, bringing me eyeball to eyeball with the most three-dimensional city in the world. Twelve years later the number 13 had shrunk to an air-conditioned single-decker. I preferred to walk or use the laughably convenient outdoor escalator. Despite the lack of democracy in Hong Kong and the ruthless power of tycoons, which made reading the *South China Morning Post* so dispiriting, there were many charms and many lessons to take back home. I was enchanted by the whispering of elderly people doing tai chi at dawn under the trees above the college. I discovered that rapid change can be energising.

If you visit China as an educator you are in luck. You meet children, parents and teachers. School visits are carefully staged but you can glimpse something of their ordinary lives. You will never be off-duty: very early starts to travel to a distant school or college, lunch at 11.00, discussions at the end of the school day when your hosts will certainly ask you to make a formal statement in response to what you've only just seen, followed by supper at 17.00, a parade of dishes to be eaten as soon as they arrive at the table, followed by several shots of Mao Tai to exchange hospitable toasts. As I sat at the round tables with Chinese colleagues I was conscious of myself in an unprecedented way but this was not disturbing. I was highly visible but also unknown, which suited me. These days were enthralling, mysterious and intense.

Teachers would always comment on my left-handedness, which was not permitted in their schools. In the UK we are obsessed with reading. In China they are obsessed with writing. It has to be done in a certain way, the same way for everyone, the fundamental sign of being truly Chinese. When we gathered in the staff room after a day observing in classrooms, they laughed and asked me how could it be that I was allowed to choose? In kindergartens I saw staff helping children with crayons and pencils. If a child picked one up with their left hand, staff would place it in the other. They would do this as many times as necessary. There was no comment, no criticism, no insult, no shaming, just attention to achieving conformity. I saw no problems arising from this attitude. No stammering or fidgeting. The children were treated with patient affection. The right hand would eventually be preferred. Perhaps the children's plastic brains adapted pretty well. There must be youngsters whose left-handedness was too strong an impulse for correction and I wondered how they would get on. Today it may be easier for left-handed people, as increasingly international food can be eaten with a knife and fork rather than chopsticks and as computers replace the need for handwriting in more and more contexts. On a keyboard you compose Chinese characters through combinations of roman letters. You couldn't have a keyboard displaying the thousands of commonly used characters. Cultural imperatives remain strong, however: one right way to draw a character, one right way to eat your food – the identifiers of being Chinese.

My partner and I travelled in China throughout the 1990s. Black Flying Pigeons weigh a ton. The bikes do not have brakes, gears or lights. We slipped into the flow along Beijing's flat city streets, joining the swathes of cyclists going to work, rice bowls and tea caddies hanging off their handlebars in a plastic bag. It felt like a belonging, two outsiders tucked here into ordinary life, insiders smiling in recognition as we puffed by. We weren't really going anywhere, only further into a new world, relying on the landmarks of a bell tower, a perimeter wall, the one new skyscraper or a blue-tiled temple roof to guide us.

In 1996 I participated in a conference in Kunming, capital of the western province of Yunnan. The university did not enjoy high status. So far from the great cities of the east coast and with many students following part-time or vocational courses, which were not at all prestigious. It was a different story with information technology, however, which was right up-to-date because of the numbers of students studying at a distance. I received my first email from Kunming.

I was in Hong Kong again the following summer, for the Handover from Britain to China. We marvelled as Elgar's 'Nimrod' rose up against the hot rain to embrace the Peak. Such misplaced beauty was mesmerising, a valediction to illegitimate true love. Around midnight on 30 June, after four drenching days, the rain finally stopped. I heard Martin Lee's speech at the Democratic Party's rally outside the Legislative Building in Central. A London-trained lawyer and trilingual Chinese patriot, he embodied the best of both worlds in that irreversible moment. If you look carefully at page two of the *South China Morning Post* for 1 July, I am there smudged in with the rest of the crowd.

On a stormy night in January 2000 the drive from Heathrow to Canterbury, where I now had a research fellowship, was long and uncharted. Juggernauts barrelling to the coast enveloped us in leaping sheets of water. My old Ford Escort strained against the cramped challenge of three Chinese colleagues plus their luggage for six months. This was the final year of my British Council partnership. As I gripped the wheel and squinted for a flash of useful road-sign I thought back to my first trip to China. In 1988 it was the Westerners who had piles of immoveable cases. I would watch with mounting embarrassment in airport arrivals halls as endlessly willing Chinese porters struggled with what must have been unfathomable items from an unimaginable world. Twelve years on it was my Chinese friends who travelled with mysteriously large numbers of bags and boxes. I took a deep breath to exit from the motorway, rushing uncertainly onto a motorway that seemed to be going south, while my colleagues cheerfully rehearsed what they knew about our destination: the Cathedral, Thomas a Becket, Chaucer. I had read the Prologue to the *Canterbury Tales* and the *Wife of Bath's* story at school. I loved the vigour of Chaucer's language and I could still recite the famous opening line. My Chinese friends, however, listed all the Tales, in order, with their main characters. They laughed at the idea that they, too, were on pilgrimage.

Between the two Dragon years of 1988 and 2000 I made eight return journeys to China, visiting and revisiting eleven cities:

Beijing, Shanghai, Guangzhou, Nanjing, Kunming, Shenzhen, Hangzhou, Suzhou, Xian, Guilin, Hong Kong.

In China I needed a calling card. Colleagues invented a name for me based on the sound of Patricia: Ba Di Sha. Not only the sound but also the meaning; a name has to be positive. There are no proper names in Chinese, they're all common nouns. As there aren't nearly as many different sounds as there are characters, you have to match them up carefully, to make sure that your overseas visitor doesn't present the wrong kind of name. My 'Ba Di Sha' means 'Beautiful White Mountain'.

Cancer

A year after my first visit to China a sugared almond appeared below my left nipple. Grey-haired and bored, a doctor slid the ultrasound block over my breast. Like a blackboard eraser but gelled, it was smooth and cold rather than dry teeth-on-edge rough. He pursed his lips but the disgust seeped out anyway. 'You must be feeling very undignified,' he said. 'No,' I said. 'I'm here to find out if that lump is cancerous.' My breast had to be examined. I had to lie down and open the clinical gown. I welcomed it. I wanted to know. What had 'dignity' to do with it? Only if you think that what's going on is the exposure of an almost middle-aged female body to the gaze of an older man who can't stay put in his professional role. He introduced the idea of dignity and proceeded to give me a low rating. As well as the anxiety of waiting to see if I had cancer I now had to cope with his revulsion. It is possible that he was trying to be sympathetic, making crass small talk to divert me away from what we were actually there to do, as if saying, 'It'll soon be over', which it wasn't. That moment of patronage and dismissal was my first encounter with the powerfully negative reactions to my breast cancer. I realised I would need energy for resistance as well as for recovery.

Seven years later my cancer returned and I had further operations. I was given a morphine pump. Severe headache and nausea made me turn it off. I discovered that I was not in much pain. 'You're so calm,' the ward nurses murmured during the slow removal of bandages, holding their breath, the ward hushed as a mortuary chapel. Hospital staff expected me to be distraught. The pain that needed relieving was theirs. For what could be worse than menopausal infertility? Single-breastedness. And she's got both! Getting rid of one fatal disease I had somehow contracted two more. The tumour was gone and forgotten as they asked: 'Is this a woman?' The answer reverberated like a drum: 'Not any more.' I became aware of a value system which holds that the absence of a breast is worse than the presence of a tumour. I began to understand the competitive power of tumours and breasts as palpable symbols of fear and desire.

Lined with shelves and colourful cardboard, the storeroom was like a high-street shop in the solemn hospital corridor. 'Sister' pulled down some boxes and we discussed what would suit me. Each box contained a single breast. To my eye and touch they could have been just-cut from living flesh, except that there was no blood. But there was warmth. For how weird would it be to have a cold breast beside a naturally heated one? There were all skin tones, all sizes, all shapes; many decisions to make before matching a fake breast to my

226

remaining original. The box itself had a Union Jack design on the lid. What did it really contain? A new life for me as a reconstituted whole woman? A prosthetic to remind me daily of my wound? Did it represent denial or bereavement? Was there nothing in between? Or any celebration of my actual situation – recovery from a life-threatening disease? My lover touched the scar with pleasure. It was my lifeline.

Site-specific

Yet here we are again. Twenty years later. On the very spot of my daughter Joanna's birth in 1980 and her first meeting with my mother, I rejoined the cancer world for a fourth time. My tumours return but they do not move. They are site-specific. Another kind of immobility – that central theme of my life.

Soon after my latest diagnosis in 2018, I went to Paris for a few days. Walking along Boulevard Raspail I saw that the inscription carved exactly a hundred years ago under a frieze on each side of the door of number 67 was 'BON COURAGE'.

The UCH Macmillan Cancer Centre is a short walk from home in Bloomsbury. I am checked and looked after. The nurse said some people don't turn up for their consultations, running away till they have no choice, but I feel drawn to it, the other world I now belong to yet again. This was a shock. After so many years. A shock but familiar. No spread. There's a drug that didn't exist twenty years ago. Only licensed last summer. New ways to shrink a tumour. Daily pills that push surgery further away. Not possible at the moment – too messy and too doubtful of success.

I talk about body parts to Katya, the young Italian nurse who does the ECGs. She never saw her mother naked. She understands the difference between being seen by a doctor and being looked at by a man. She agrees that too often they are the same person. She would find it hard to relax on the examination bed.

I listen to people in the waiting room. The woman sitting next to me one day was wearing a face mask and talking to her mother on the phone. 'I've go to be completely healthy,' she said. 'I can't have any infection.' I couldn't hear her mother's response but then the woman said, 'See it as an opportunity to de-clutter, what suits the new house rather than what suits you.' A mask against infection to help her get through cancer, her mother moving into a care home at the same time. Turns out the woman in the mask is a new mother herself. She holds up her phone. 'Here's my beautiful little baby,' she says through her mask to the woman sitting on the other side.

The drop-in centre at the hospital is called The Living Room. A euphemism, though this is not how it feels. These days it's more like a new truth. Many of us live with cancer, which becomes a significant other, a second person, a conversation's other half.

As I walk across to Huntley Street, I can't help thinking of Joanna, born in the leap year of 1980, and the 1920s maternity hospital demolished to make way for the cancer centre. Joanna has just had a baby herself. I wish my mother were here to meet him. For I think of her, too, coming to the old building to meet Joanna for the first time. She wore her best tweed coat and a soft hat. She leaned round the curtain by my bed to say hello to Joanna. Cycles of life on the pivot of this one place. My lifecycle shaped by a single place on my body, too: my left breast, above my heart, alongside my writing hand.

When I re-registered at the centre, they commented on my hospital number – U/EH 4241. 'It's very old,' they said. Nowadays the identifiers are longer and there aren't any letters. Mine dates from the fifties: tonsils out at seven, broken leg set at twelve, then radiotherapy at forty-two, all treated in the long tentacles of the red-brick Waterhouse building behind the glass and bronze centre built on top of the place of Joanna's birth. Specific places transformed by reconstruction.

I resisted reconstruction for my body. 'Good,' said my surgeons in 2018. The first time I had cancer I decided to have a lumpectomy, the minimal option, given that the tumour was so obvious, well defined and near the surface. When cancer returned, seven years later, the tumours were again obvious but not at all well defined: my nipple leaked, I had patches of mottled rough skin and an area that was hard and white. A mastectomy, then. Still not a major operation. Still contained within this outside-body-part of me.

When my 1996 surgeon visited he raised the possibility of a reconstruction, not routine in those days. It would have transformed the procedure into something much more serious, lengthy and painful. My doctor wanted to help me retain my sense of full womanhood. That was his genuine, sympathetic, male perspective. I didn't accept that single-breastedness would diminish my womanhood. I didn't want to pretend I'd never had breast cancer. I was also concerned that a reconstruction would mask any further recurrence, buried under new layers of organic and artificial material, and delay a vital diagnosis. This is what happened to the mother of a nursing sister I met in a South London A & E, whose reconstructed breast prevented the discovery of a recurrence till it was too late. This might well have happened to me, either in 1998 or in 2017. During the planning of my most recent operation, the thoracic and the plastic surgeons both emphasised the benefits of not having a reconstruction. Before they even began on their tasks of excising the tumours and rebuilding my chest wall and outer layers, they would have had to spend time removing the fake breast, unnecessarily extending the already long operation and throwing away material that would otherwise be positively useful now.

Mother and daughter

Cancer returned for the first time just as Joanna was writing her GCSE exams. I put off telling her for a few days, till the last one was finished. She came bounding out of school that summer afternoon, free and smiling, up into the park where I was waiting for her at the café. We hugged, for the good news and for the bad. Twenty years later my fourth recurrence was confirmed at the same time as her pregnancy. 'You can join me on my sofa, then,' she said. 'That's where I'll be. Better than sitting on your own sofa down there by yourself.'

Joanna and I shared her sofa. We went out walking arm-in-arm. We went swimming together, as I had with Rachel in South London two years earlier when she was pregnant. Watching their long bulbous bodies cruising through the water was the most hilarious treat. Now, we, mother and daughter, had tumours and babies growing inside us. Joanna is doubly alive. I am too, of course, for cancer is exceptionally alive. She is heavy and apprehensive. I am light-headed and apprehensive. Our breathing is getting shallower and more conscious. We might have been in hospital at the same time, being relieved of what was growing inside us: the best and the worst. But plans for me have changed, extended to at least the autumn now. Joanna's baby, a boy, was born in the Whittington Hospital near her home on 1 March 2018, my father's 110th birthday.

After a walk up the hill and down into Crouch End, we reflected on becoming mothers in our thirties. We both feel this was positive, that it was the right time for us, even though we'd been with our partners for years before having children. But there was a crucial difference I hadn't appreciated till now. Joanna and Josh are settled into their careers. Looking back to our early days of parenthood, I realise that, despite the relative maturity of age, my husband Alex and I were both at the beginning of new careers. He was a scientist but switched to art history and was in his first full-time humanities job. I was trained as a history teacher, then worked for the Inner London Education Authority. After a second first degree, in psychology and philosophy, I worked on a PhD thesis challenging common assumptions about teenage thinking. Now it hits me. How personal this was.

I was unconscious of it then, too close to my own teenage years, too focused on being a rigorous researcher. The youngsters I taught were mistakenly, often insultingly, portrayed in official reports and casual conversations. My concern arose from deep discomforts.

Then I saw the advertisement for a new post at the Open University. The job description matched my background and experience. Here was an opportunity to begin a late academic career. Between the interview and starting work, however, I conceived Joanna – pregnancy in parallel with a completely new working world. After three months' full maternity leave the following spring, I half-worked and half-fed, my right breast growing larger than my left as I sat at the kitchen table with my colleague and my baby, planning and writing. Now, I sit on Joanna's sofa with my grandson and my tumour. My body's under attack but I feel fine. My mind is sound but there's a lot going on in there too.

My friend Andrew says, 'Let's call it small-c.'

What's changed?

Not enough. 'You're so calm!' they cried all those years ago when they encouraged me to pump the morphine and anaesthetise myself against the loss of breast and womanhood. 'That's a nice shirt,' said a male doctor this time. At once I was back with the doctor and his ultrasound block thirty years ago, saying, 'You must be feeling very undignified.' What had my shirt got to do with it? Only if your reflex is to console women who face recurrent breast cancer and further de-womanly disfigurement. The words spoken gently. As a compliment. Reassuring. It wasn't that nice a shirt. Light blue M&S. I don't dress up for a medical examination. Why would I, when it would be completely beside the point?

After her treatment for breast cancer, journalist Joanna Moorhead was invited to a make-up session. She was angry. How could it possibly be relevant? As a diversion maybe, when she might have been feeling low. Expected to be feeling low, that is, as a damaged woman, perhaps needing a decorative consolation. It was assumed that make-up would cheer her, make her feel more feminine, sexy and attractive after the onslaughts of breast cancer would destroy these attributes. Feeling cheered by decoration is fine but Moorhead seems, here at least, to understand how weak it would be as cancer-consolation.

Moorhead's article (*Guardian* 'Journal'. 10.7.19) was triggered by the offer of bell-ringing, an imported American ritual to mark the end of your serious illness and treatment. I shared her anger at the cosmetics and the bell-ringing, which could be particularly thoughtless for women whose cancer later recurred. I share her anger at the use of battle cliches to describe the experience of cancer and I agree that fear and anger can be very close. I do not share her wish to deny that she's had cancer and return to her daily life as if it never happened. Her subsequent emphasis on cancer as life-changing seems inconsistent.

In an earlier article Moorhead discussed her refusal to have a mastectomy and here she displayed a more straightforward sensibility (*Observer Magazine*, 4.2.18). Like me, she found a lump near her left nipple, which, like me, was diagnosed as a Grade 2 cancer. This was 'devastating'. Yes. But as I read her article, I felt a great distance open up between us. For her, the breast was the really serious problem, an anxiety reinforced by her female surgeon's warning that 'this will change your life'. Moorhead writes: 'cancer, I thought, I could deal with, losing my breast I could not.' How would I 'feel about my new body?' She has four daughters and she tells us that she fed each of them for three years. I also breast-fed my daughters, though not for as long. Clearly Moorhead's sense of herself is truly bound up with her breasts. She loves them, the literal expression of her motherhood and her sexuality, as 'essential' as her heart and lungs. 'My big fear was that I'd be diminished by a mastectomy, that I'd never again feel whole, or truly confident or comfortable in myself' and 'My mental health was at risk'. Moorhead wanted the cancer gone but wanted her sense of herself intact. As if these were bound to be incompatible. She accepts the tragedy of single-breastedness, according to which a mastectomy is 'detrimental' to a woman's sense of 'self, femininity and sexuality'. What about the rest of her body? Or the other ingredients central to a female sense of self, sexuality and confidence: her mind, her spirit, the sound of her voice, her energy, the way her body moves?

Journalist Moorhead acknowledges that 'others take their lead from' her and in the later article she makes it clear she's writing solely about her own experience. Awareness of the responsibility does not lead her, here, to reflect on the different ways to be a woman, feminine or fulfilled sexually. Instead, she reinforces her own fear by generalising: 'Many women who've had mastectomies do find it difficult to reconcile themselves to the body they inhabit after surgery.' She doesn't search for possible answers to 'Why?' When she writes that 'breast cancer, after all, won't kill me', the implication is that losing a breast might.

Moorhead has her life's experience, I have mine. They are significantly different, though our breast cancer began in the same place. She feels proud, whole, in control, her femininity and sexuality not diminished. I do not feel proud or a need to be in control and femininity has never been central to my 'sense of self'. My sexuality was not diminished through being single-breasted. My mastectomy came during the years of my greatest sexual fulfilment. My scars are signs of life. I reject Moorhead's view of what makes a whole woman. We are both women. For the woman that I am, losing a breast was trivial.

Cancer came before and after the end of my twenty-year marriage. Was it the cause? This was the view of my ex-husband. I partly agree. My view of what cancer means has evolved since 1989. As has my view of what happened between us. There were the time-consuming satisfactions of childcare and work to push us apart. We were older parents and just starting second careers. Later there was, for me, the re-emergence of music-making and writing projects, collaborating closely with new friends. There was China, too, of course, adding its powerful distance, a dozen years of my life that I began to see as my first real break with 'home'. I'm not sure now that even the Far East, where I enjoyed a totally new visible-invisible relationship to people and places, represented a real change. Is this what cancer means for me? In a life of persistent continuities, so unlike the lives of my parents, has cancer been my first experience of true discontinuity?

December 2018

My thoracic surgeon arrived with a flourish, as if on horseback, with sparkling hooves and shining helmet under his arm, to give the upbeat speech on the eve of battle, energy compressed for a knightly charge down the corridor with pennants flying.

This fourth time, my site-specific cancer needed several operating teams. After all the previous surgery there was no flesh left for it to burrow into. It clung to a rib. The breast-cancer surgeon began with an exploration of my lymph-nodes, then came the excision of the rib, then the plastic surgery to fill and cover the gap. Eight hours of strenuous work for them. Eight hours of anaesthetic for me.

Up on the intensive care ward, now topped up with painkillers, I was delusional. This was routine. My specialist nurse checked to see if I knew where I was. Yes and no. I saw hovering figures clustered in a semi-realistic scenario that my dope-soaked brain organised into a story of people come out to play at night, fantastical but recognisable. I was there, too, so how would I get back home? My brain kept whirring. A few days later when the door of my room on the main ward was open I could see the outside panel, reinforced and painted dark blue to withstand regular knocks from equipment wheeled in and out. I sat in my chair and saw the scuff-marks become figures drifting along a Munch waterside, softly juddering like the nocturnal crowds down in special care.

At a check-up a few weeks later, my plastic surgeon examined the scar slanting up my back and round to the front in the shape of an oval. His handiwork, of course, but I knew he was right when he smiled and exclaimed, 'Fabulous!

This is where I come from

My mother and father met in 1930, when she was eighteen and he was twenty-two. In their wedding photos they're smiling, happy. They are not touching. He couldn't stand up and give her a hug. They couldn't go out dancing. He couldn't stand up and kiss her at the same time. They would both have fallen over. When my father told his *Woman's Hour* listeners he believed in hands-off parenting, it was literally true. He couldn't embrace us, or even hold our hand, though we did sit on his lap when we were small and he played a sort of 'Catch!' as we ran past his armchair. He couldn't come out walking with us or take us for a drive. Ma drove us to the White City or the Cameo Poly cinema or the Festival Hall, dropping us off then picking us up later. We could go walking with Dad in Suffolk when he propelled his chair slowly along the lanes. My youngest brother Christopher was the most regular companion during those years, which is where he heard family stories not told round any table. By that time I was a teenager and off on my bike in the other direction.

In the online, global twenty-first century, it is hard to appreciate the dominance of print journalism and the BBC in British life in the mid-twentieth. These were the years of my father's 'active service'. They were the high points of his career, despite the recurrent undertow of responsibility without power that took such a toll at home as well as at work. Colleagues described him as an 'alien' and a 'cripple'. My father described himself as a 'cuckoo'. He was both 'hero' and 'humble servant'. He had travelled that huge distance from the impoverished North East to Oxford, Printing House Square and St James's. He was witty, irascible, tolerant, never pompous. He was a Casualty of Peace.

My mother was capable and tireless but not confident, feeling 'constrained' by her upbringing, physically awkward in public. Like my father, she was a child when her own father died. She endured the cutting short both of an academic career and then of her public life in education and local politics. As well as the moves she and Donald made, for his career and due to the war, her large family also kept her increasingly indoors. She was defensive when she saw daughters enjoying careers and children. If we 'left' them to go out to work, was that an abandonment and a reminder of her own lost opportunities? When we asked her to tell us about her life, she said, 'Don't bully me.'

My mother had three interrupted careers. This has only become clear to me after paying proper attention to her life. I knew that when they were living in Essex she was elected as a Rural District Councillor and served as a College Governor and that this public life ended when they moved back to London in 1951. Recently, I discovered that she completed substantial work on a postgraduate research project ten years earlier. Her subject was Tudor economic history, expanded from the distinction of her undergraduate thesis, supervised by my father. This, as well as her Hampshire WEA evening-class teaching, was cut short by their move to London at the beginning of 1937, when Donald became Assistant Editor of the *Economist*.

A third career was interrupted by the war. In her *Reminiscences*, my mother told us how much she enjoyed her brief time with the John Lewis Partnership from 1937 to 1938. She worked in the new Peter Jones, in the china and glass departments then in personnel. She loved the diversity of colleagues and the security of the partnership structure. However, she joined the Auxiliary Territorial Services (ATS) in 1938 and was called up a year later. The ATS was full of petty irritations but, as with John Lewis, she relished the camaraderie and her contribution to the war effort: instructing young girls who'd never been in a car to drive and maintain vehicles not remotely designed to serve as ambulances. My father's journalism was his 'active service'. This was hers.

Could my mother have continued in at least one of her careers: academic, local politician and public servant, John Lewis manager? Even with all the moves in and out of London? Even with all the children? Was she already so overwhelmed by the summer of 1951 that the idea of a professional life for herself seemed ridiculously distant? Probably. She didn't say.

When I was a teenager there was talk of Ma doing some teaching and I think she did make a few enquiries. By then the money would have certainly made a difference, though I didn't know that. But her training and experience were so long ago. She was strong-minded but she was not a performer. Instead, she became involved in regular voluntary work with the Family Planning Association. She loved it, though she wasn't the best person to discourage young women from having lots of children.

The verbs of family life were reading, writing, fighting. There was no censorship of opinion at home. We could ask any question we liked. My parents would never say 'don't speak to me like that', pulling rank to avoid discussion. But they were reticent about their own lives, hardly any personal storytelling, no photographs from the years before we were born. Most inhibiting for me was their over-reaction to the smallest problem, so different to the progress of their early life together. As a teenager this effectively shut down what could have been my maturing attempts to face practical or emotional difficulties. I never witnessed any problem-solving. Not even a light bulb changed. I had to learn from a friend how to change a plug when I took my record player to university. Dad would hold up his hand and say, 'It's fine', which I interpreted as permission and support, from the other side of the room. My mother would say, 'It's late', by which she meant let it go, have a rest, stay here, not dismissive but to avoid anguish. She needed to keep her children within sight but she couldn't abide confrontation. And she couldn't count on my father for any help. She opened Pandora's box and, as she once confessed to her sister, out sprang five 'formidable' children.

The Parents and the Children

My father saw women as people. This was the basis of his wartime articles on the value of women's contribution and of his respect, throughout his career, for female colleagues. At home, they were 'the parents', we 'the children'. No gendered adjectives were used to distinguish one from another. I accept that it was important for my father to have a son to name 'Harry' in remembrance of his brother killed in 1943 and that my mother felt something special when that son, Robert Harry, was born, despite being ill after the birth and the simultaneous move from Essex to London being so fraught. I see that I was lucky not to be the sibling just above or just below.

Home life was, for me, a relief from the enduring pressures of 50s femininity that permeated a school supposed to be more enlightened. It's true that Anne was small and blonde and that we fought. I would say it was because she was so controlling. But I can admit that it was also because smallness and blondeness seemed to make life so much easier. There was still only one way to be. The time came when you

The parents, the children

had to take off your socks and put on your stockings, complete with suspenders attached to a rubbery roll-on. This rite of passage was as problematic for me as the impossibility of 'flying-up' from Brownies to Guides but there was no way out. Now we can choose. I can put the socks back on. Tights are for weddings only. I watch in amazement as women are stepping back into corsets, that Ms Spandex is a millionaire.

I know my mother and father better now than I did when they were alive. I feel closer to them and more separate. I understand for the first time just how far my life has been affected by my father's immobility, how strange was my normal. This profoundly influenced the ways we behaved towards each other. Bodies and appearance were unimportant compared to the reading, writing and fighting. Emotion was often channelled in a parallel ding-dong of words and noise that you couldn't call 'talking' or any sort of 'exchange'. In recognising the absence of physical intimacy at home, I can't help thinking about other intimacies: my father's view of himself as a man, my mother's view of herself as a woman. However intractable the tensions later on, 'the children' were vital to their re-created lives. I am more like my mother, who was large and awkward, though she could be tough-minded and elegant. Like her, I am fearful of other people's over-reaction to stress. Like Dad, I am intolerant of bragging and affectation. I am attracted to the anonymity that was his habitual cloak. My last 'wild rage' was when I struck out at him as a sleep-deprived new mother after some cutting remark he made to Ma.

Writing about ourselves

My mother wrote her *Reminiscences* in the 1980s, encouraged by my sister Mary after Dad died, a brief but invaluable memoir alive with stories and strong feeling. Years earlier Mary proposed making a study of my father's career in journalism. His response to her was a letter, long and careful as always. He concluded:

> I think the task is too daunting. I wrote hundreds and hundreds of pieces. I remember a few of them specifically and those I remember are not necessarily the best or the most important. My role was always editorial. I wrote as much of my best stuff into other people's (anonymous) pieces as I did in my own (anonymous) ones. Good luck, but don't blame me if the marathon is too much.

Was Dad ever tempted to reveal himself while still, of course, writing anonymously? There are clues. Dad's desk was in the bay window of my parents' bedroom in the West End Lane flat, high up overlooking communal gardens. This is where he wrote book reviews for the *Economist*, every fortnight from the late 1960s to his last month. It was light up there but I know he felt trapped. He wasn't well. He was lonely. He couldn't get up and walk about, stretch his legs. But when it came to a job, with a deadline, he remained utterly professional, concentration and commitment enduring as his health and spirits declined. Here was his own life, reflected back to him from the pages of memoirs and biographies of politicians, economists, journalists and historians he had known thirty or forty years before.

In one review he described Lloyd George, another man whose father died young, as a spoiled, charming user of people, and 'like almost everybody who is deposed or retired from the top before he is old (he was fifty-nine when he left off for good) he would not again risk the hurly-burly for fear of being put down.' Dad was fifty-seven when he left off for good.

Reviewing Christopher Hibbert's book on London, my father asked, 'Are we still so ashamed of what we build now and so inordinately proud of all that we used to build, that our Hibberts cannot come to terms with today or tomorrow?' He was always on the side of change. And he was always prescient. Reviewing two books of 1981 on the press and broadcasting, he wrote, '...what disappoints the grateful reader is again...the old-fashioned conclusions. Like it or not, British newspapers are going to be transformed by the new electronic means of production and distribution; and television and radio are going to be changed even more by the chances and choices offered by satellite transmissions and by cables. These authors shrink from facing the future.' My father had no nostalgia for the world of his youth.

The sub-heading above of one of my father's *Economist* book reviews from the 1970s is 'Blood is thicker than Biography'. He'd been reading the memoirs of a pair of press barons and he concluded that family dynamics would always bleed over and obscure a well-judged story, that the emotions would always be too strong. I recognise the bulimic quality to all this. If we started, would we ever stop?

Writing about my parents and how they shaped my growing up I realise that the strong but invisible ties between us can look deceptively like detachment. We occupied different spaces, we were not open to each other and didn't touch each other. My father couldn't carry anything. Indifference to possessions was not a choice for him. Except for books. Even books he did not revere as objects. This would make us disinclined to pick them up and read them. He would never put books in a cabinet with doors. The only objects he treasured were the first he ever owned: the bookcases, desk and chest he had made in Southampton. And later the oak table he bought second-hand for his Surbiton bed-sit during the war. A few popular books the only things handed down from his parents or grandparents.

It is fashionable these days to draw on objects to link parts of a story, to propel the story. In his memoir *The Hare with Amber Eyes*, Edmund de Waal uses the family collection of Japanese netsuke to construct the thread of his account, as if they would make the chunks of history and memory more compelling. Similarly, Jean Vautrin's 1999 novel about the Paris Commune of 1871, *Le Cri du Peuple* (translated as *The Voice of the People*), uses the glass-eye tokens exchanged by criminal gangsters to shape the characters' stories into the arc of a hunt. Netsuke and glass eyes or other kinds of object-links can work, or they can be shoehorned in and feel artificial, or they're impossible, as in my life. Atmosphere was the binding element in my upbringing: intense, frustrating, entertaining, unnerving. So when literary people cry: 'Where's your narrative drive?' I imagine a Chandleresque thriller, noirish as befits a family saga, and I hear the scrunch of gravel on Narrative Drive, up in the Hollywood Hills, the lone gunshot, the intoxicated starlet and a car rolling downhill with no brakes.

When I am in Westleton I don't often visit my parents' grave. The flint church stands beyond an arch of lime trees. Diamond light filters through the east window. I move from the shade of the tree's enormous branches towards the chronology of the village. In various stages of erosion, inscriptions fill the graveyard. On my parents' headstone, however, there are no adjectives to sustain their memory. This might be intriguing to someone new to the village, sampling its

245

ecclesiastical history or waiting for the pub across the road to open. And perhaps this was the only way to do it. Aside from the expense of stone carving there was also the impossibility of agreeing on a choice of words. Between my sisters, my brothers and myself, there's no single understanding of our parents' personalities, behaviour or commitment to us. Within our shared amniotic there are profound differences of experience, perception and life-long feeling. You would need a headstone for each child and a sweep of outsize graffiti. Five spray-cans for all the love and hate and unanswerable questions. Contradictions carved in stone.

My family life was like a classical drama where significant action takes place somewhere else and an account is given to the audience by a messenger. Except that the messenger never arrived in North London. The reality was an atmosphere, quiet or full of suspense, nerve-wracking or hilarious. Intellectually permissive, socially anxious. Now I know that my unreflective adolescent years coincided with my father's most difficult years at work. There were signs: exhaustion, silence, sudden outbursts, his poor head for alcohol. But there was no telling. He was there and not there. My attention was elsewhere. His attention was elsewhere. We sat in different rooms.

What if I had pushed through the open door of my upbringing? Would I have become the sort of young woman whose desire to be feminine cancelled the androgynous qualities that helped me through breast cancer and still be me? My adolescent self has emerged as a separated twin. I look back at her with my old ambivalence. I realise how much I owe her.

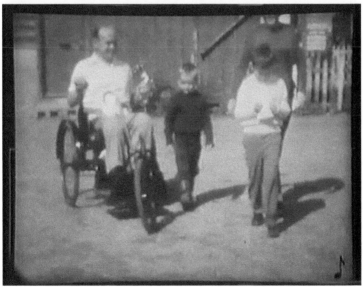

Donald in his chair, taken from home movies

Self-portrait

light falls from the left
onto the page below
the page is my face
this is what I do

onto the page below
I make myself with words
this is what I do
from the inside edge

I make myself with words
without telling you my name
from the inside edge
of the family room

without telling you my name
I write at the open door
of the family room
where bodies crush and shout

I write at the open door
like a separated twin
where bodies crush and shout
stuck in the long shadow

like a separated twin
I search for my old-young self
stuck in the long shadow
of fifties heartiness

I search for my old-young self
as light falls from what's left
of fifties heartiness
to the page which is my face

Acknowledgements

Angela Thirlwell has read every word of every draft and given me constructive critical comments on the content and structure of this book throughout the years of research and writing.

Christopher Tyerman has read and commented on drafts at different stages and given me detailed advice about the writing. He is also a mine of family stories, including those heard on walks with my father as he rode his three-wheeler round the Suffolk lanes when I was a teenager and off somewhere else on my bike.

David Kynaston has read and commented on drafts of the book and given me generous advice and encouragement.

Judith Ravenscroft has read and commented on the book as it evolved and given me valuable support.

Special thanks to my cousin Roy Tyerman for giving me permission to use invaluable photographs and other documents in his possession, as well as passing on family stories that only he knew.

Thanks to Philip Astor for sharing documents about my father's career discovered during his own memoir research.

To Ruth Dudley-Edwards for granting me access to interview transcripts made during her preparation of *The Pursuit of Reason*, published to celebrate the *Economist*'s 150th anniversary, and for support and encouragement during the preparation of this book.

To Louise North at the BBC written archives, Caversham Park, for discovering files on my father's extensive contributions to radio and television hitherto unknown to his family.

To Ellen Tout, at the North Yorkshire County Record Office, Northallerton, for gathering together resources on the history of the places of my father's childhood.